FAMILY
STRESS
MANAGEMENT

FAMILY STUDIES TEXT SERIES

Series Editor: RICHARD J. GELLES, *University of Rhode Island*
Series Associate Editor: ALEXA A. ALBERT, *University of Rhode Island*

This series of textbooks is designed to examine topics relevant to a broad view of family studies. The series is aimed primarily at undergraduate students of family sociology and family relations, among others. Individual volumes will be useful to students in psychology, home economics, counseling, human services, social work, and other related fields. Core texts in the series cover such subjects as theory and conceptual design, research methods, family history, cross-cultural perspectives, and life course analysis. Other texts will cover traditional topics, such as dating and mate selection, parenthood, divorce and remarriage, and family power. Topics that have been receiving more recent public attention will also be dealt with, including family violence, later life families, and fatherhood.

Because of their wide range and coverage, Family Studies Texts can be used singly or collectively to supplement a standard text or to replace one. These books will be of interest to both students and professionals in a variety of disciplines.

Volumes in this series:

1. LATER LIFE FAMILIES, Timothy H. Brubaker

2. INTIMATE VIOLENCE IN FAMILIES,
   Richard J. Gelles & Claire Pedrick Cornell

3. BECOMING A PARENT, Ralph LaRossa

4. FAMILY RESEARCH METHODS, Brent C. Miller

5. PATHS TO MARRIAGE, Bernard I. Murstein

6. WORK AND FAMILY LIFE, Patricia Voydanoff

7. REMARRIAGE, Marilyn Ihinger-Tallman & Kay Pasley

8. FAMILY STRESS MANAGEMENT, Pauline Boss

9. DIVORCE, Sharon J. Price & Patrick C. McKenry

10. FAMILIES AND HEALTH, William J. Doherty & Thomas L. Campbell

Pauline Boss

FAMILY
STRESS
MANAGEMENT

FAMILY STUDIES **8**
TEXT SERIES

By their example, Verena and Paul Grossenbacher taught me about managing family stress—in good times and in bad. They struggled with the effects of immigration and the Great Depression, simultaneously seeking challenges in community leadership and service. They taught me that life without stress is dull. To them, my first teachers, I dedicate this book.

—Pauline Grossenbacher Boss Riggs

Copyright © 1988 by Sage Publications, Inc.

For information address:

SAGE Publications, Inc.
2111 West Hillcrest Drive
Newbury Park, California 91320

<table>
<tr><td>SAGE Publications Inc.
275 South Beverly Drive
Beverly Hills
California 90212</td><td></td><td>SAGE Publications Ltd.
28 Banner Street
London EC1Y 8QE
England</td></tr>
</table>

SAGE PUBLICATIONS India Pvt. Ltd.
M-32 Market
Greater Kailash I
New Delhi 110 048 India

Printed in the United States of America

Library of Congress Cataloging-in-Publication Data

Boss, Pauline.
    Family stress management.

    (Family studies text series; 8)
    Bibliography: p.
    Includes index.
    1. Family—United States—Psychological aspects.
2. Stress (Psychology) I. Title. II. Series: Family
studies text series ; v. 8.
HQ536.B69   1987   306.8'5'019   87-23302
ISBN 0-8039-2380-5
ISBN 0-8039-2381-3 (pbk.)

FIRST PRINTING 1988

Contents

Preface

SINCE 1973, I have formally studied family stress. It began with clinical observation, then moved to a process of theory development, hypothesis testing, reformulation of theory, and back again. From the beginning, I was interested in perception: how the family as a whole (and individual members) perceived what was happening to them. What you read here is primarily theory, a book of ideas to be tested.

Not only should you, the reader, test these ideas professionally, but you should also question them personally. I hope there is validity in this book for your own perceptions and family experience.

Perceptions growing out of my own family experiences are undoubtedly woven into this book. In spite of the scientific method and good clinical training, we are not always objective. David and Ann Marie Boss were in junior high school when I first started researching family stress; they are now grown up and away from home but still giving me feedback when my ideas about family stress do not make sense. I hope that never stops. This, too, is part of the theory development process.

Acknowledgments

I AM INDEBTED TO Dr. Richard Gelles, editor of this series, for his confidence, support, and helpful reviews; to David Klein, to Sandra Burge, Ph.D., for reviews of earlier drafts; to Sylvia Rosen, editor, for her sharp mind (and pencil); and to Nanette McCann for her skill and patience in typing the manuscript.

I am also indebted to Dudley Riggs, who believes in teaching through art and humor. With his creative suggestions, Gordon Smuder illustrated this book. Ann McQuinn consulted on this project.

For assisting on research projects from which this book draws, and for wrestling ideas with me, I thank Jan Greenberg, Ph.D., Debra Pearce-McCall, A.B.D., Wayne Caron, M.A., Joan Horbal, B.A., and Susan Herloffson, and Ann Garwick.

For providing financial support for research on midlife family stress and boundary ambiguity, I am indebted to Richard Sauer, Keith McFarland, and M. Janice Hogan, Minnesota Agricultural Experiment Station (grant MIN-52-048 and MIN-52-049). Gratitude is also expressed to the National Institute on Aging for support of my research on family stress from Alzheimer's disease (grant 1P50-MH40317-01).

Finally, to the hundreds of families I have heard from through survey research, in-home research, and in family therapy; and especially to the families of men still missing in action, who were the first, I want to express my deepest appreciation.

Introduction:

The Family—Stress Reducing or Stress Producing?

The family should be a refuge, a place to find rest and comfort from the problems of the world. Sometimes, however, the family is a source of even more tension. Rather than a refuge, it becomes a prison from which to escape. For most of us, however, the family is neither a haven nor a prison; it is neither the solution to all problems nor the cause of everything that goes wrong. Reality lies somewhere in between.

This book is addressed to students of family science and to professionals who work with stressed families. Its focus is theory for the practitioner. The phenomena revealed in clinics often become the starting point for research that expands theory, and theory, in turn, enlarges the capacities of clinicians to diagnose and treat and of educators to teach. It is safe to say that some stress—too much or too little—is the root of most family problems.

Definitions are very important. It is only when everyone uses terms to mean the same thing that we can understand each other. Thus definitions are given considerable attention in this book. They not only clarify the meanings of words but also the relations among the various concepts. In Chapter 1, then, I introduce and define three fundamental terms in family stress theory: family, stress, and system. In addition, I discuss some theoretical concepts that are the basis of my approach to family stress. In Chapter 2, I introduce and define terms and concepts that are directly related to family stress.

To make it easier to keep in mind major ideas, a list of points to remember is presented at the end of each chapter. Their purpose is to summarize the contents of the chapter and to list those ideas that must be kept in mind as one reads on.

CHAPTER

1

Setting the Stage

THE CURRENT TREND to romanticize the family, to talk only about its strengths and achievements, is of great concern to me. When we sentimentalize the family, we ignore the pressures it is under in our changing world. Doing so not only denies that family stress is real, but discounts the fact that certain family stresses are not always bad. Some forms of stress can keep family life lively and fun.

A more realistic approach is to recognize that families today are under a great deal of pressure, more than ever before. One just needs to follow a family around for a few days to see their need for stress management and problem-solving abilities in order to survive. Some of the daily problems with which they must contend are traffic (unlike anything our grandparents ever saw); threats to life and property (few communities are free of potential or actual crimes); expectations for children (they must achieve in order to be accepted in the middle-class world); emancipated sons and daughters who move back home (because of unemployment or divorce); and both parents working outside the home (that's what it takes to keep up mortgage payments these days). Good child care has become a luxury that few working parents—especially single parents—can afford, so that work and family tensions are higher than ever before.

Most important, perhaps, is the loss of leisure; there is less and less time for couples to relax together or to spend time with people they care about. Family life has *not* gotten simpler for present generations; it is *more* complex and the pace is faster. Economic and psychological pressures are high—for some families, overwhelming. This is a fact that family professionals must face if we want to help families to stay strong.

Family stress management, therefore, becomes a major challenge to families today. In my work as a family therapist and family stress researcher, I have come to the conclusion that the families in trouble are often *not* sick families; they are those that simply are unable to deal with the volume of events they are facing. *They are not sick families; they are just highly stressed.* It is not always possible for families to avoid the events that cause problems. Being stressed does not necessarily mean a family is weak; it may simply mean that they are in a threatening situation. A bad farm economy, for example, cannot be blamed on the family, nor can chronic illness, nor job transfer. Too often we blame the family for its troubles; yet, even during "good times," it is not always possible to avoid problems in family life.

Rather than focus on how to avoid family stress, which is neither realistic nor even desirable, my objective is to share with you the accumulated theory on the causes, characteristics, and management of family stress. I do not include lists of steps detailing how to manage the stress; many "how-to" books are already available. What I offer is a book that is designed to help you to *understand* the process of recognizing and managing those events and situations that cause high stress in families.

In providing the fundamentals of family stress theory, my assumption is that the world is not always a fair place and even strong families can break down. In itself, it is not always bad for families to come apart; in fact, sometimes it is therapeutic. Such families usually recover and become strong again. What I provide here, then, is an understanding of why some families go under and why some survive. My basic premises are that (a) not all families are the same; (b) not all events that stress families should be viewed the same; and (c) not all families have the same values and beliefs. Differences must be looked for and taken into consideration.

FAMILY STRESS DEFINED

Much has been written about individual stress. Hans Selye, M.D., was the first and most prolific writer on individual stress. He was the first to define and measure stress adaptations in the human body. As a result of his research, he believes that "stress is the common denominator of all adaptive reactions in the body" (Selye, 1978, p. 64). He defines stress as "the state manifested by a specific syndrome which consists of all the nonspecifically-induced changes within a biologic system."

The family's degree of stress results from events or situations that have potential to cause change. Stress is change; by itself it is neither good nor bad; it depends on how the organism (in this case the family) reacts to it. (See also Antonovsky, 1979; Dohrenwend & Dohrenwend, 1974; Lazarus, 1976; Lazarus & Folkman, 1984; Mechanic, 1978; Monat & Lazarus, 1977; Selye, 1980.)

Family stress is defined as pressure or tension in the family system. It is disturbance in the steady state of the family. It is normal and even desirable at times. It is inevitable because people (and therefore families) develop and change over time. With change comes distur- bance, pressure—what we call stress. Family routines change, patterns of interaction change, people are born and people die. Even in the larger societal context, changes occur. The Great Depression, World War II, the civil rights movement, the women's movement, and the searing polarization caused by the Vietnam War, all caused changes. Such events in the larger context cannot help but create stress inside the family system.

DEFINING THE FAMILY: A MATTER OF BIAS

The definition of *family* used in this book is as follows: The family is a continuing system of interacting personalities bound together by shared rituals and rules even more than by biology. Ernest Burgess, one of the original family social psychologists, defined the family as a "unity of interacting personalities" (1926/1968). I add to this definition, "and the personalities must have a history and future together for shared rituals and rules." In my definition of the family, although I do not place more emphasis on the sharing of rituals (weddings, birthdays, gradua- tions, holidays, funerals, and so on) than I do on the sharing of biology and genetics, I recognize that in our present society, biology no longer is the single determinant of "family." Children of divorce and adopted children are most aware of this fact (see also Adams, 1986).

Clearly, my definition of the family runs counter to the legal and more traditional definition of the family as an isolated nuclear unit: two parents living with their offspring under one roof with father earning the living and mother taking care of children and home. I do not agree that this one form of family is the keystone of American society and that, if it changes, all of society is in danger of coming apart. On the contrary, I see *change* in the family structure as necessary and life enhancing.

Family professionals and policymakers must recognize and accept change in the family structure and try to enhance rather than impede such change. However they define themselves, most families mobilize to find their own solutions to problems. But a rigid, monolithic definition

"OF COURSE IT'S STRESSFUL!
THATS WHY I DO IT!!"

Figure 1.1

of family prevents family problem solving in times of trouble. Let me give as an example the case of *Moore vs. City of East Cleveland, Ohio* (1977; see also Boss, 1979).

The City of East Cleveland, Ohio, in an official housing ordinance, defined the family in a way that brought about the arrest of Mrs. Inez Moore in 1973. Mrs. Moore, age 62, was sentenced to 5 days in jail and fined $25 for violating the city's 1966 zoning law that limits occupancy in a single-family house to the head of the family, his or her spouse, parents, one married child, and that child's children. She had taken into her large house her divorced son and his small boy, and also her other grandson from a widowed son. Although this absorption of two nuclear families by the grandmother, who owned a large house, helped to relieve the stress caused by a death in one family and divorce in the other, the city officials called this grandmother's solution illegal because more than one family was now living in her house.

Mrs. Moore could not see the logic in a law that offered such a narrow definition of the family; so she decided to fight the city. She lost in every court in which she challenged the ordinance, including the Ohio Supreme Court. The Ohio Supreme Court agreed with the city. Mrs. Moore then appealed to the U.S. Supreme Court. Her attorneys argued that the ordinance violated her right to privacy and that East Cleveland was guilty of heavy-handed intrusion into the privacy of the American family. On May 31, 1977, the U.S. Supreme Court voted five to four to reverse the previous decisions, saying that the East Cleveland ordinance "makes a crime of a grandmother's choice to live with her grandsons."

In the majority opinion, Justice Lewis Powell said that the U.S. Constitution's protection of the family's sanctity does not stop at the arbitrary boundaries of the "nuclear family." History and tradition show that the family extends to a larger household in which many generations may live together.

> Especially in times of adversity, such as the death of a spouse or economic need, the broader family has tended to come together for mutual sustenance and to maintain or rebuild a secure home. This is apparently what happened here. Whether or not such a household is established because of personal tragedy, the choice of relatives in this degree of kinship to live together may not lightly be denied by the State. (413 U.S. 495)

This case illustrates my point. Defining the family only as a nuclear structure does not fit with the reality of many American families who must find their own way to manage stress and solve problems. Mrs. Moore, a grandmother, helped two nuclear families by combining them into an extended family. Her solution should be applauded.

I cannot support the point of view, therefore, that only one kind of family is normal and only one way to manage stress is right. A less monolithic view of the family and of family stress theory is presented here to take into account the rich diversity of American families. If family stress theory is to be useful, it must be broadened to include *all* types of families and varying types of solutions to their problems.

When I write about family stress, I am aware that, for me, *family* has always meant more than "isolated nuclear family." I grew up in a Swiss immigrant extended family. In addition to my parents and siblings, it included grandma, uncles, and hired hands (and even the school teacher during a blizzard). We all lived in one big house on a farm. When my siblings and I grew up and left home, we continued to live in the same small community but in separate houses within a 5-mile radius. Crossover between household boundaries was frequent. Doors were not locked; children frequently played with cousins; sisters babysat for each others' children; grandparents always helped out young families and welcomed grandchildren for visits; meals were often shared; and money was exchanged as gifts or loans. In short, my family stretched into a *modified extended family system* so that, although not all members lived under one roof, all were inside one family, symbolically as well as by self-definition. Celebrations reflected that definition because all these people were included.

I use the term *family* to mean an extended system: parents, grandparents, sisters and brothers, aunts and uncles, nieces and nephews, and cousins, as well as persons not biologically related, such as in-laws, godparents, and even persons who live and grow up within the family or who join it later in life. This sort of flexible family boundary is often found in immigrant families and in minority American families. Flexible family boundaries enable families to survive, especially in economically harsh or hostile environments.

My own family is no longer in a harsh environment but we still maintain a modified extendedness and celebrate the same rituals together. Family members are spread across the United States; they live in single-family dwellings, condos, dormitories, or apartments, but all keep in regular communication via telephone, airplane, train, and automobile. A happy event is immediately shared by telephone. If there is unexpected trouble, an immediate call results in plane reservations and regrouping wherever help is needed. This is not an unusual pattern for many American families today.

GENERAL SYSTEMS THEORY:
THE FAMILY AS SYSTEM

Families are living organisms. This means that families have a structure, symbolic as well as real; they have boundaries to maintain; instrumental and expressive functions must be performed, thus ensuring the organism's growth and survival.[1]

Systems theory states that the system is greater than the sum of its parts. In families, this statement means that the collection of family members is not only a specific number of people, but also an aggregate of particular relationships and shared memories, successes, failures, and aspirations. Each family has a unity of its own.

In family stress theory, consequently, systems theory helps us to understand why one person has a particular response when he or she is alone but another when the kids come home from school, Dad comes home from work, or a grandparent arrives for a visit. The stress level of the *whole*, in other words, is qualitatively different from the sum of the individual stress levels of the family members. Alone, each person in the family may act cheerfully and in control; together, however, they may create an atmosphere of anger and depression.

Family therapists and health care professionals have witnessed a powerful collective quality when there is a sick child in the family. There is a ripple effect when a parent overfocuses on that child in the subsequent reaction of a sibling (or mate) who feels left out. The family member who feels neglected begins to distance himself or herself or to act out for attention. A sibling may run away; a mate may indulge in self-destructive behavior or have an affair. Even getting a series of speeding tickets can be an example of such attention-seeking behavior by someone who feels abandoned in family interactions. Too often professionals and researchers look only at the person who is acting out although, in fact, the stress is present in the *whole* family system. Sometimes the family's stress is vented in the behavior of one person; this member is said to act as a scapegoat for the rest of the family system. Finding a scapegoat within the family is one way families protect themselves from change. Systems tend to want to stay the same; yet stability is not always functional. A family may look fine but, if even one person in it is depressed or in trouble, then the system needs to change.

THE CONCEPTUAL FRAMEWORK:
SYMBOLIC INTERACTION

Because the perception of an event (the meaning of the event to the family) is central to my approach to working with stressed families, the basic conceptual framework is symbolic interaction. Symbolic interactionism is a school of thought in social psychology.[2] It focuses on *interaction* within a family and on symbols of interaction (e.g., language or rituals). The idea is that a stressed family constructs a symbolic reality based on shared meanings and role expectations inside the family. Those shared meanings, however, are influenced by the world outside the family: the community, the society, and the culture. This larger context provides the "shoulds" and "oughts" (technically, the norms and mores) for individual families. From the symbolic interaction perspective, one can say, therefore, that a family's rules reflect the rules of its larger context. However, when a family belongs to a minority subculture that, within the culture of the larger context, adopts different rules, the family experiences even more stress because of the members' efforts to solve their own problems in their own way. Inez Moore's experience is a good example.

While I was studying family stress, it became apparent to me as both a researcher and a therapist that unless I could identify, understand, and measure *symbolic* interaction, I would not have a true picture of what was happening in stressed families. Thus during my initial studies of the families of men declared missing in action (MIA) in Vietnam, I paid as much attention to the stories the wives told to me as I did to the computer printouts that summarized responses to my questionnaires. Although the latter were easier to analyze and much more acceptable as research at that time, it was the stories told by family members that informed me of the reality of *symbolic interaction*. Let me share one of these stories:

In 1973 I was a member of the team at the Center for Prisoner of War Studies in San Diego studying families of men declared missing in action. In pretesting a 3-hour questionnaire another interviewer and I (both of us clinicians) sat with the wife of a navy pilot who had been shot down over Vietnam several years earlier.

I read from the questionnaire: "Do you believe your husband is alive?" Her answer was immediate and clear. "No, not anymore." I was surprised by her clarity. I already believed that perceptions were a key factor in understanding family stress, but I was not prepared for her frank answer to my question. She went on. "But he did come to see me twice after he was shot down. The first time he met me in front of our house right outside here on the lawn. He told me to sell the house and move to a neighborhood with a better school. He also told me to sell the car and get a station wagon since the children were getting bigger and I would need the space." She paused and then went on. "I did these things—it took me about a year. Then one day, my husband came back for a second visit, this time in the bedroom, and we were alone. He said I had done a good job on making all these changes and that he was proud of me. He wanted to tell me that he would be leaving for good now and that he wanted to say good-bye. He said he loved me, he was proud of me, and I should marry again if I wanted to."

We were silent. She had tears in her eyes as she told that story. I believed it. She had constructed reality for herself and her children in a way that was functional. Later I learned that she had grown up on an Indian reservation and this was how her people dealt with the sudden loss of a loved one. Who was I to tell her that her story was not valid? It was her reality based upon the "symbolic interaction" between herself and her missing husband.

When families are in stress, one hears many such stories. The idea of boundary ambiguity (discussed in Chapter 4) grew out of similar stories that I listened to in a family therapy clinic in Wisconsin and the summaries of universal concepts about what actually stresses families. For me, as a researcher, the symbolic interactionist perspective made it possible to recognize new data about families in stress. But the process has only just begun. As family researchers, educators, and therapists work together more closely, family interaction based on symbols will be assessed in new ways. Perception becomes critical to the understanding of family stress.

THE DILEMMA OF WHERE TO FOCUS
IN WORKING WITH STRESSED FAMILIES:
THE FAMILY OR THE INDIVIDUAL?

One of the arguments in family research is about whether families have a distinctive quality apart from the individuals making up the family. Is there such a thing as "a family perception" or "a family response"? Both researchers and clinicians alike have reported observing this phenomenon of family paradigms (Reiss, 1981). One often sees what we might call collective delusions in families—for example, families that have a deaf member ("He can hear when he wants to") or alcoholic members ("No, Dad is not an alcoholic, he just drinks to relax"). Sometimes a member must leave a deluded family system before he or she can perceive the actual reality. Away from the group, one sees more clearly the weaknesses and strengths of the family system. While one is in it, there is an implicit agreement on what is considered real, on what is perceived as stressful, and on the rules for continuing the denial. When such family delusions give way, change is made easier for the individuals in that system.

PERCEPTIONS

In this book, therefore, I assume that a family system has a character of its own and that this unity produces the variable, *family perception*. It does not, however, preclude paying attention to each family member's perceptions. Family perception and individual perceptions frequently are not the same. Both are needed to get the full picture. The focus on the family system should not come at the expense of individuals within that system. Both *individual* and *family* data are needed to understand family stress; unfortunately, family data only recently have been added to stress literature.[3] And even more recently, individual differences, primarily gender, are also being included.

The United States of America is a diverse society made up of families that mostly come from other countries. The "melting pot" has not occurred. American society consequently is a collection of diverse family units-more like a salad than a uniform mass. When family therapists, educators, and researchers work with stressed families, this diversity becomes clear.

I often listen to families describe their problems, and I am constantly surprised at how different their assessments are from mine. *Diverse backgrounds give us diverse perceptions.* Thus I believe that understanding the families' perceptions of stressful events (as a whole and individually) is basic to understanding their stress level. The meaning they give to the event is the key to their appraisals of the situation; this meaning influences not only the families' vulnerability but, also, how the families and family members will act and react to what is happening to them. Only after professionals see the event through a family's own eyes can we know how to assess, support, and intervene, if need be.

For more than a decade, I have studied families in stress to determine their perceptions so that interventions could be developed to reduce vulnerability. I have worked with some families as a researcher, with others as a therapist, and with still others as an educator. Because of my work, it follows that this book has a research, intervention, and

"WHY CAN'T EVERYONE SEE
THIS THE WAY I DO?"

Figure 1.2

prevention orientation. In other words, I am defining a common language of family stress management that can be used by researchers, clinicians, and educators.

THE BIGGER PICTURE: A CONTEXTUAL APPROACH TO UNDERSTANDING FAMILY STRESS

If family stress is defined as an upset in the steady state of the family, then not all stressed families are necessarily in trouble. Other factors beyond the stressful event also influence family vulnerability. I propose here that the end result of the stress process (whether the family and its members manage to avoid or survive crisis) is influenced by the family's *internal and external contexts*. The first context is composed of dimensions the family *can* control, the second, of dimensions the family *cannot* control (see Figure 2.1). This contextual model is discussed in Chapter 2.

Although I build on current research and on the work of Reuben Hill, I have moved in a new direction, first, by taking this contextual approach and, second, by including clinical as well as research data to support the importance of perception and symbolic meaning.[4] A new variable—family boundary ambiguity—is presented in Chapter 4 to illustrate this point.

THEORY BUILDING

My aim over the past decade in working with stressed families has been to search inductively for more general variables. It has been a search for "umbrella variables" that would produce *a useful family stress theory to help a variety of troubled families*. My aim is to broaden the base. Toward that end, I have attempted to define terms carefully, to examine new and general variables of a more qualitative nature, to discuss past and current research, and, above all, to place family stress into a context so that the theory will be more useful to a wider population of therapists, teachers, nurses, doctors, researchers, and policymakers who work with stressed families of different ethnic backgrounds and beliefs. Good theory, after all, must be useful in explaining and predicting family stress for more than just one kind of family.

Family stress theory, I believe, is at an impasse right now because we have relied too heavily on only one source of information: the empirical. Empiricism is indeed necessary to test variables, but first we have to identify valid variables. We still do not know all the critical variables in family stress theory. To be sure, we now are beginning to know empirically what family therapists always have known: that *the family's perception matters*. But we still do not know what all the indicators of that perception are.

Theory building is a process that starts with ideas, testing them empirically, reformulating and testing again (if necessary), and then drawing conclusions. But the most important part is the beginning: the ideas or insights.

HOW TO READ THIS BOOK

I hope you will read this book not just for facts but also for ideas and insights. Be aware of the feelings and memories about your own family that surface as you read. These are data also and are very important to your understanding of *family stress theory*. They will make the book more real for you. The symbolic interaction perspective places a high value on one's own perceptions; hence your perceptions become part of the experience of reading this book and part of the information I provide. I highly recommend that you talk about and discuss the contents with others as you go along.

HOW THE BOOK IS ORGANIZED

Chapter 1 is an introduction that explains the theoretical perspective from which I have developed ideas about family stress. Chapter 2 presents definitions of important concepts and terms, but is more than a glossary. In a sense it maps out the territory the rest of the book covers. Nevertheless, the concise definitions of terms are available for reference as you read remaining chapters.

Chapter 3 focuses on the popular concept of coping and presents some cautions about it. Chapter 4 discusses the core idea of the book: that the family's perception of the event is critical in determining how and if they can survive. It is in this chapter that a specific example of family perception is introduced as a new variable in family stress theory—that of boundary ambiguity.

Chapter 5 adds, explicitly, the concept of denial to family stress theory. This important concept always has been included in the literature on addiction and dying but, to my knowledge, it has not been formally incorporated into family stress theory until now. Chapter 6 completes the discussion of the family's internal context with an examination of family values and belief systems. Family members' values and beliefs are influenced by the larger culture but they are viewed here as they appear in the internal world of the family.

The outside world of the family is discussed in Chapter 7. Although less space is devoted to the external than to the internal context, both are critical for understanding family stress. I hope this chapter will stimulate colleagues in anthropology, history, macroeconomics, biology, medicine, developmental psychology, and sociology to see how micro and macro views of family stress can be meshed. Chapter 8 discusses the conditions of victimization and their interaction with family stress theory. Chapter 9 looks at the past and the present. After reviewing the history of family stress theory, focusing specifically on Reuben Hill, I speculate about where the field is today and where it may be heading.

Overall, this book is intended to do more than review literature about families in stress. It is intended to make you think, ponder, feel, remember, hypothesize, and test. In the final analysis, when we think about families and stress, our own experiences become a part of that process.

POINTS TO REMEMBER

(1) Family stress is inevitable, but not all stress is bad. Stress usually happens to families: The family is threatened by an event that creates a situation that is beyond its control at the moment.

(2) Family stress management is a major challenge to families as well as to family therapists, educators, and researchers.

(3) Not all families are the same; not all events that stress families should be viewed the same; and not all families have the same values and beliefs.

(4) Stress is "the state manifested by a specific syndrome which consists of all the nonspecifically-induced changes within a biologic system" (Selye, 1978). The family's degree of stress results from events or situations that have potential to cause change. Stress is change; by itself it is neither good nor bad; it depends on how the organism (in this case the family) reacts to it.

(5) By definition, the family is a continuing system of interacting personalities bound together by shared rituals and rules even more than by biology. There is no such thing as one kind of "normal" family.

(6) In *Moore vs. City of East Cleveland, Ohio* (1977), the Supreme Court accepted the principle that the term *family* may be defined to include extended kin such as cousins and grandparents as well as parents and children.

(7) Systems theory holds that the system is greater than its parts. However, if even one member of a system is in trouble, then the whole system needs to change. A family system has a character of its own; this unity produces the variable "family perception."

(8) Perception is an important variable. It determines how an event is viewed by a family (as a unit) as well as by individual members of a family. Perception, therefore, affects the level of stress the family feels.

(9) The same event is not viewed the same way by all the people in

one family, by all families in one community, or by all communities in one society. Perceptions among *families* differ; perceptions among *family members* differ.

(10) Symbolic interaction focuses on the interaction within a family and on the symbols of interaction (e.g., language). A family constructs a symbolic reality on the basis of shared meanings and role expectations.

(11) Family stress cannot be studied apart from the larger context in which the family is living.

NOTES

1. The expressive role is to communicate and be in charge of feelings and emotions in the family; the instrumental role is to make decisions, be in charge of business matters, discipline children, and earn money. Talcott Parsons wrote that males were to perform the instrumental roles in families; females were to perform the expressive roles (Parsons & Bales, 1955). Such rigid separation of roles in families makes the family vulnerable to stress. I believe families are strengthened if *both* males and females in the family can perform *both* instrumental and expressive roles.

2. Wesley Burr, a family sociologist who takes this perspective, has written more technically about symbolic interaction, which is also known as interactionism, symbolic interaction, role theory, self theory, and social behaviorism.

> Whatever label is used, it is the brand of social psychology that emerged from the writings of William James, C. H. Cooley, and George Herbert Mead. Technical readers will recognize that there are slight differences in emphasis in some of the different traditions in this theoretical orientation. For example, the dramaturgical approach used by Goffman (1959) differs from the more formal approach used by Biddle and Thomas (1966); and the more quantified methodology used by some is different from the more qualitative approach suggested by the older University of Chicago approach typified by the work of Strauss and Blumer. These subtle differences can be ignored for the purposes of a text that focuses on the application of the basic ideas of this school of thought rather than the discovery and justification of new ideas. (Burr, Leigh, Day, & Constantine, 1979, p. 102)

3. This emphasis on individual as well as group indicators denotes a social-psychological perspective in this book.

4. In presenting family stress from a contextual perspective, I have used induction as well as deduction. Induction, according to family stress theorist Wesley Burr, is "logical movement from the specific to the general" (1973, p. 20). The process of induction is especially important in theory building because it allows discovery of more general propositions that encompass and explain a range of specific propositions. Deduction, on the other hand, is logical movement from the general to the specific. It is the process of using general propositions and other identifiable conditions to explain why specific propositions or conditions exist (Burr, 1973, p. 19). One deduces from general theory to specific hypotheses, whereas one induces from specific observations to a general theoretical level.

FURTHER READING

Adams, B. (1986). *The family: A sociological interpretation* (4th ed.). New York: Harcourt Brace Jovanovich.

Antonovsky, A. (1979). *Health, stress and coping.* San Francisco: Jossey-Bass.

Boss, P. (1987). Family stress: Perception and context. In M. Sussman & S. Steinmetz (Eds.), *Handbook on marriage and the family.* New York: Plenum.

Bourne, P. G. (1969). *The psychology and physiology of stress.* New York: Academic Press.

Brown, B. B. (1980). Perspectives on social stress. In H. Selye (Ed.), *Selye's guide to stress research.* New York: Van Nostrand Reinhold.

Bruhn, J. G., Chandler, B., Miller, M. C., Wolf, S., & Lynn, T. N. (1966). Social aspects of coronary heart disease in two adjacent ethnically different communities. *American Journal of Public Health, 56,* 1493-1506.

Buckley, W. (1967). *Sociology and modern systems theory.* Englewood Cliffs, NJ: Prentice-Hall.

Burr, W. (1973). *Theory construction and the sociology of the family.* New York: John Wiley.

Dohrenwend, B. S., & Dohrenwend, B. P. (1974). *Stressful life events: Their nature and effects.* New York: John Wiley.

Goldberger, L., & Breznitz, S. (Eds.). (1982). *Handbook of stress: Theoretical and clinical aspects.* New York: Free Press.

Kellam, S. G., Ensminger, M. E., & Turner, R. J. (1977, September). Family structure and the mental health of children. *Archives of General Psychiatry, 34,* 1012-1022.

Kutash, I. L., Schlesinger, L. B., & Associates (Eds.). (1980). *Handbook on stress and anxiety.* San Francisco: Jossey-Bass.

Laing, R. D. (1969). *The politics of the family.* New York: Pantheon.

Lasch, C. (1977). *Haven in a heartless world.* New York: Basic Books.

Mechanic, D. (1978). *Students under stress: A study in the social psychology of adaptation.* Madison: University of Wisconsin Press.

Monat, A., & Lazarus, R. (Eds.). (1977). *Stress and coping.* New York: Columbia University Press.

Moos, R. H., & Billings, A. G. (1981). Conceptualizing and measuring coping resources and processes. In L. Goldberger & S. Breznitz (Eds.), *Handbook of stress: Theoretical and clinical aspects.* New York: Macmillan.

Olson, D. H., McCubbin, H. I., Barnes, H., Larsen, A., Muxen, M., & Wilson, M. (1983). *Families: What makes them work.* Beverly Hills, CA: Sage.

Parsons, T., & Bales, R. F. (1955). *The family socialization and interaction process.* Glencoe, IL: Free Press.

Pearlin, L. I., Menaghan, E. G., Lieberman, M. A., & Mullan, J. T. (1981). The stress process. *Journal of Health and Social Behavior, 22*(4), 337-356.

Pogrebin, L. C. (1983). *Family politics.* New York: McGraw-Hill.

Price, V. A. (1982). *Type A behavior pattern.* New York: Academic Press.

Rahe, R. (1974). The pathway between subjects' recent life changes and their near-future illness reports: Representative results and methodological issues. In B. S. Dohrenwend & B. P. Dohrenwend (Eds.), *Stressful life events: Their nature and effects.* New York: John Wiley.

Reiss, D. (1981). *The family's construction of reality.* Cambridge: Harvard University Press.

Reiss, D., & Oliveri, M. E. (1983). Family stress as community frame. In H. I. McCubbin, M. B. Sussman, & J. M. Patterson (Eds.), *Social stress and the family*. New York: Haworth Press.

Selye, H. (1978). *The stress of life* (rev. ed.). New York: McGraw-Hill.

Selye, H. (Ed.). (1980). *Selye's guide to stress research* (Vol. 1). New York: Van Nostrand Reinhold.

Stinnett, N., & DeFrain, J. (1986). *Secrets of strong families*. New York: Berkeley Books.

Thorne, B., & Yalom, M. (Eds.). (1982). *Rethinking the family*. New York: Longman.

Von Bertalanffy, L. (1968). *General systems theory* (rev. ed.). New York: George Braziller.

CHAPTER

2

Definitions:

A Guide to
Family Stress Theory

FAMILY STRESS TERMS AND MODELS have not always been used consistently in the literature of family research and practice. My goal is to clarify definitions so that therapists, educators, and researchers can all understand each other in their mutual goal to help families manage stress. You may find it useful, therefore, to think of this chapter as a glossary of family stress terms and a theoretical map. As you read, you may want to refer to this chapter since definitions and models will not be presented as fully again (see Figure 2.1).

Families do not live in isolation; they are part of a larger context. This becomes critical to understanding the family stress management process. I propose that there are two different contexts in which family stress is mediated—one in which the family has control and one in which it does not. I explain these contextual maps and then move on to family stress definitions. Throughout, keep in mind that I present stress as change and change as stress. These terms are used synonymously and with neutral connotations. More is said about this usage later in this chapter. For now, think of stress as change. It can range from drastic to mild, but whether it is good or bad for the family will be determined by the multiple elements in the family stress management process.

THE FAMILY'S EXTERNAL CONTEXT

The external context is made up of components over which the family has no control (see Figure 2.2). It includes the environment in

28

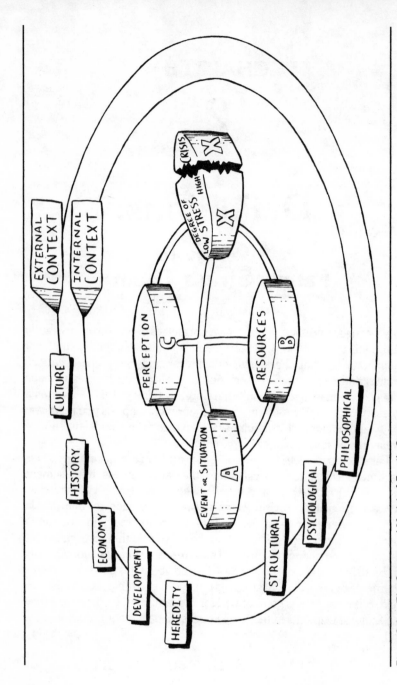

Figure 2.1: The Contextual Model of Family Stress

which the family is embedded, also called "the family's ecosystem." However it is labeled, the family's external context is here because it consists of the constraints of development and genetics as well as economics, history, and culture. In short, we are talking about the "time" and "place" in which a particular family finds itself. The external context cannot be ignored in explaining family stress, outside the control of family system itself, and has tremendous influence on how the family perceives events and manages (or fails to manage) whatever stress is produced.

Past research has shown that the cultural context (the place), for example, is a strong determinant of whether and how families will manage stress (for details, see Boss, 1987). In cultures that tend toward fatalistic belief systems, such as India and Turkey, families may be less likely to harness a flooding river than would families in a more mastery-oriented culture such as the United States. Currently we are in the "age" of technology, and U.S. families rely more heavily on human-made solutions to all problems. Our confidence in technological mastery over even natural disasters is nowhere clearer than in Palo Alto, California, where the delicate Stanford Linear Accelerator was built directly over the San Andreas fault. When I asked why they were taking such a chance, the engineer answered that their technology could overcome any earthquake.

Such thinking epitomizes the belief that we can control nature, a mastery orientation that is predominant in mainstream American culture. There are subcultures in our country, however, such as the Native American, in which mastery is not valued so highly and the use of our technology is minimal. Surely such a cultural context influences how a family deals with the stressful events that may occur over its life cycle.

Let us turn now to components of a family's *external* context as they appear in Figure 2.2.

Historical Context

The historical context of family stress is the time in history in which the event occurs to the family. I referred above to the age of technology in which we find ourselves now in the 1980s. This context influences our family life today. When we talk about family stress, we have to know what historical events are influential at the time. For example, if the stressful event is loss of a job, it would mean something different if the loss happened in 1929 after the market crashed (the prelude to a

30

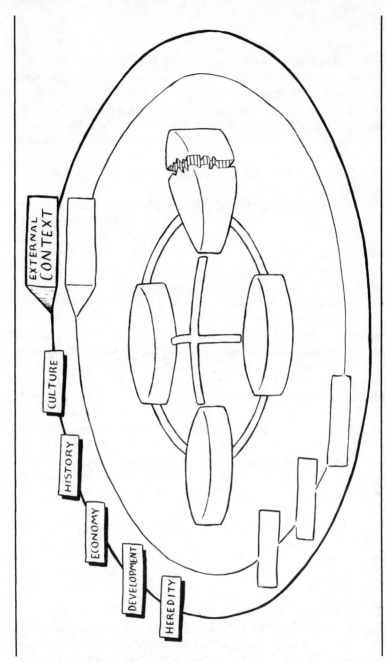

Figure 2.2: The Contextual Model of Family Stress: External Context

EXTERNAL CONTEXT

CULTURE

HISTORY

ECONOMY

DEVELOPMENT

HEREDITY

worldwide depression), and another thing if it happened during the post-World War II years (a time of full employment), or after technology revamped American industry, with robots replacing many assembly line workers and with Baby Boomers flooding the work force.

Ascertaining the historical context identifies the climate in which a stressful event occurs to the family. We then know if the event occurred in a climate of choices or in one of discrimination and limited resources. The answer will show the historical influence on how a family deals with stress. Glen Elder (1974), a sociologist who studied children of the depression of the 1930s, found that the men and women who grew up with marked scarcity tended to resort to similar strategies (frugality, conservation) to manage stress. We will find other such cohort effects as we incorporate into our analyses the time in history when the family exists.

Economic Context

The community's or society's economy forms the family's economic context; the state of the economy influences how the family reacts to a stressful event. For example, during a strong economic period, being laid off from a job is not as serious to a family as it is when the economy is weak; when unemployment is high and jobs are scarce, the chance of getting other work is slim. In northern England, for example, as on the Iron Range in Northern Minnesota, some families have been without a paycheck for several years. Unemployment is not due to the family breadwinner's lack of skill or ambition but, rather, to the obsolescence of iron mines and factories. Here, of course, we see the combined effects of the age of technology (a historical context) and the economic context. They cannot always be separated. One influences the other.

Developmental Context

The developmental context for the family is the stage in the life cycle of both the individuals and the family when the stressful event occurs (see Papalia & Olds, 1986; Aldons, 1978). A family may be new even if the people in it are old. Marriage and remarriage occur at every age, not just during youth and early adulthood. Even pregnancies now have a wider range within the developmental context. The event of pregnancy undoubtedly is viewed more positively by the families of a couple in their thirties than by the families of a couple still in their early teens. The different levels of family stress caused by the same event (in this case pregnancy) can be explained by developmental context. The developmental context in which an event occurs mediates the perception of events as much as the event itself. Whether we as individuals are old or young matters in how we perceive and manage an event; and whether the family as a unit is new or old matters in how the event is perceived and managed.

Hereditary Context

The family's biological and genetic context affects the health and physical strength of the family members. Some people, and therefore families, because of genes and good constitution, are simply stronger than others. Such families have more stamina and resilience when under pressure. As a result, they not only have more energy to deal with an event, but also the strength to persevere and continue dealing with high stress, when the stressful situation is of long duration (chronic). A strong constitution makes it easier to act in defense of oneself and one's family when stressful events occur, and especially when pressure continues over a long time.

Cultural Context

The cultural context consists of the predominant ideas, values, and ideals that give a distinct character to the larger society in which the family lives. Although the family's private beliefs and values are under their control and therefore part of the internal context, the cultural context provides the canons and mores by which families define the way they live. The cultural context also defines the larger society's rules for problem solving, management styles, and accepted methods of managing stress. The larger culture, then, provides the rules by which the family operates at its micro level.

Sometimes, however, a family belongs to a subculture (e.g., minority or ethnic group) that has its own rules, and these rules may conflict with those of the prevailing culture. The incongruity between the rules for problem solving in a family's subculture and those in the mainstream culture may be the reason that ethnic minority and immigrant families are often highly stressed.

THE FAMILY'S INTERNAL CONTEXT

The five dimensions of the family's external context just discussed impinge on a family's internal context. But, unlike the external context made up of elements over which the family has no control, the internal context is made up of elements that the family *can* change and control (see Figure 2.3). Because of this ability to change, we can begin to see why and how even highly stressed families survive and perhaps even thrive.

The *internal* context of the family is made up of three dimensions: the structural, the psychological, and the philosophical. Note on Figure 2.3 that these dimensions make up the inward ring around the core that is the family stress process.

The *structural* context refers to the form and function of the family boundaries, role assignments, and rules regarding who is within and who is outside those boundaries. When the boundary of a family is ambiguous (boundary ambiguity), there is a lack of clarity in the structural context of the family and the occurrence of stress. (Considerably more is said on boundary ambiguity in Chapter 4.)

The *psychological* context refers to the family's perception, appraisal, definition, or assessment of a stressful event. I prefer the term *perception* because it embodies both cognitive and affective (feeling) processes. The way a family perceives an event essentially determines its ability to mobilize defense mechanisms when that event occurs. In a subsequent section of this chapter, we will see how families use the psychological mechanism of *denial* to avoid facing the reality of an event that goes on for a long time, such as the terminal illness of AIDS. (See also Chapter 5 for a more detailed discussion of denial.) In the long run, the use of denial by a family or even just one member of the family blocks the resolution of the problem and the necessary subsequent reorganization of the family as a whole. I shall say more about perception throughout this book.

The *philosophical* context of the family refers to its values and beliefs at a micro level. An individual family, for example, can live by rules that are different from those of the larger culture to which they belong. Certainly, minority families in American culture experience this difference in such areas as child rearing, care of the elderly, and gender roles. When the larger culture, for example, provides government support for the institutional care of elderly parents but not for care within the family home, the external and internal contexts are brought into conflict and even more stress is created. The military subculture sometimes imposes rules on family dependents that are inconsistent with the larger culture, leading to additional stress for those families. The complexity is even greater for military families living on bases in foreign cultures. They must know and follow intermittently the rules of American mainstream culture, the military subculture, and the foreign

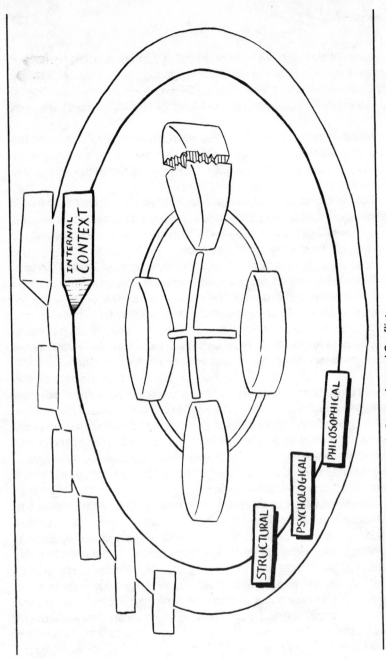

34

Figure 2.3: The Contextual Model of Family Stress: Internal Conflict

culture in which they reside. It takes a strong family to synthesize such diversity into their private philosophy.

Population mobility also creates pockets of philosophical diversity. We can find within almost any American city or town a range of family beliefs that sometimes are in direct opposition to each other. For example, some families may believe that illness can be overcome by modern science and technology; other families may put their trust in folk remedies; and still others may put their trust in the healing powers of religion. We also find some families who believe that fighting back actively is the appropriate response to a stressor event and other families who believe in passive acceptance of whatever comes their way.

Although such family beliefs and values are influenced by the larger cultural and religious context, a family's internal synthesis of beliefs and values into its *own* philosophy directly influences the family's perception of a stressful event. The internal context, more than the external, is under a family's control, and thus even within the same cultural context, families may differ in their private philosophies, and they are certain to differ in internal beliefs if they come from external contexts that espouse different cultural values.

In this book, consequently, I focus on the micro level, not because the internal context is more important than the external, but because the internal context is more malleable and under each family's control. Those of us who work with and study stressed families must ascertain each family's internal context before we can understand and assess what that family is experiencing when it tries to manage stress. To complicate matters, however, the family's internal context may change over time or individual family members may disagree in their perceptions and descriptions of the family's internal context. The very complexity of such situations calls for a qualitative approach in eliciting information about families in stress. This means family researchers and professionals must rely on each family *member's* story and each *family's* story as much as on large survey studies in which data are combined into averages.

THE ABC-X OF FAMILY STRESS:
A FRAME FOR DEFINITIONS

When Reuben Hill formulated his ABC-X model (Hill, 1958), he provided a substantial base for the scientific inquiry of family stress. He presented this succinct model to a group of social workers in 1957. With that historical presentation, Reuben Hill linked the work of family sociologists to that of clinicians. His framework for family stress theory focuses on three variables:

A—the provoking event or stressor,
B—the family's resources or strengths at the time of the event, and
C—the meaning attached to the event by the family (individually and collectively).

These three variables are the foundation of family stress theory even today. Indeed, the C factor is what I focus on in this book because, from a clinical perspective, the family's perception of an event is a powerful, if not the most powerful, variable in explaining how the family defines and reacts to a stressful event. Even though perception has been difficult to measure and, therefore, is the least investigated variable in the model, I persevere and hope that this book will encourage further investigations of the phenomenon of family perception.

Hill's ABC-X model is used here heuristically and is the center of the family stress model (see Figure 2.4). When we move in new directions, it is helpful to know where ideas fit in relation to a familiar model. Note that I do not define and discuss them in their original order. In this chapter, I focus on the A factor (stressor event) and the X factor (stress and crisis). In Chapter 3, the B factor (resources) is defined in relation to coping theory and research. The C factor (the meaning of the event) is further discussed in terms of the family's boundary (Chapter 4), denial (Chapter 5), and belief systems (Chapter 6).

Inasmuch as theoretical definitions directly affect research and clinical strategies, it is essential to be clear on how terms are used. Although I am most familiar with family stress literature, I also cite *individual stress* theorists because of their valuable contributions to our understanding of stress. Using a general systems perspective, I have merged both sets of literature. Both individual and group indicators are important to comprehending and predicting the outcome of the family stress process.

STRESSOR EVENT (STRESSFUL EVENT)

A stressor event is an occurrence that is of significant magnitude to provoke change in the family system. A stressor event is *not* synonymous with stress. Unfortunately, the literature is not always clear on this point. It is an *event* that marks a possible starting point for a process of change and subsequent stress in the family system. By definition, then, a stressor event is an event that has the potential to cause change in the family because it disturbs the status quo.

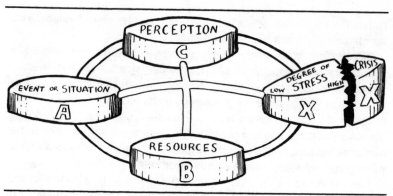

Figure 2.4:   The ABC-X Family Stress Model
SOURCE: Hill (1958).

The event also has the potential to raise the family's level of stress, although it does not necessarily do so every time. The *degree of stress* caused by the event depends not only on the actual magnitude of the event but, also, on the family's perception of that event. Families often see the same event differently (e.g., one family may be ecstatic over a move to a new city while another is panic-stricken or angry). Or the *same* family may perceive the same event differently over time (e.g., the first family move was exciting and small children were not disturbed; after the twelfth move in 15 years, however, the mother feels defeated, and high-school-aged children, angry).

A Caution About Defining What a Stressor Event Is

Keep in mind a fact I stated earlier. What is defined as a stressor event is highly influenced by the family's external context: the time in their lives and the place in which they live. In some cultures, usually those that are more agrarian, a teenaged couple having a baby would not be a cause of high stress; it could, in fact, be viewed with joy. There is one more hand to help on the farm. Community and cultural context thus influence even what the family defines as a "stressor event." Other examples of events that might be defined differently by different families are marriage, death, an adolescent leaving home, the loss of a job, flunking an exam, or even winning a lottery. We cannot automatically assess such events as stressful without first asking the family how *they* define the event. There are times when a death is a stress reducer rather than a stressor event; this reaction is often found in families in which a member has been in a coma for a long time.

Although in itself neutral, then, a stressor event has a potential for change and, therefore, a potential for creating stress levels that must be managed if crisis is to be averted. Both positive and negative events can be stressors. Winning a lot of money has as much potential to cause stress in a family as losing money. However, stressor events do not always increase stress to a crisis point. Stressor events can occur, the status quo of the family can be upset, but the family's stress level can be managed if the system finds a new equilibrium.

On the other hand, when a stressful event (e.g., sudden loss of income) happens, a family can refuse to acknowledge the event or to change their behavior (habits of spending freely, in this case). They go on as if nothing happened, using credit cards, and going deeper and deeper into debt. Here, the family's denial of the stressor event (loss of income) prevents change and thereby increases chances for crisis in that family.

The thesis in this book, however, is that the outcome of a particular stressor event depends on the family's perception of that event. A family cannot begin the management of stress or the problem-solving process until they recognize that they have a problem. Families cannot deal with a stressor event until, as a group, they recognize that the event has occurred. (More is said about denial as a barrier to stress management in Chapter 5.)

The Danger of Circular Reasoning

One more point must be emphasized in the definition of a stressor event. Because a stressor event is only a stimulus, it cannot be synonymous with the *outcome* of that stimulus. What this means is that a stressor event is not the same as the degree of stress the family experiences (see Figure 2.4). Were they the same, we would have a tautology (circular reasoning). A tautology is an untestable hypothesis because obviously "stress equals stress" or "change equals change." The correlation would be 100%. A researcher would be wasting time to try to test such hypotheses.

To avoid the danger of tautologies, I propose instead that *type of stressor event* influences *the degree of stress experienced*. Thus in the model in Figure 2.4, "type of event" equals "degree of stress" (rather than stress equals stress). This is a very important point. It avoids circular reasoning. You will see how that equation becomes even more complex (but still testable) when we add "the family's perception of that event."

CLASSIFICATION OF FAMILY STRESSOR EVENTS

Stressor events are varied and multiple. Because it is essential to be able to identify them, the basic types are classified and defined in Figure 2.5 for quick reference and better understanding. When one is faced with a stressor event, either as a professional who works with stressed families or as a family member, it is important to identify the type of event before one makes an assessment of or a response to the situation; the reason is that the type will influence the entire process: the family's perception of the event, the degree of stress experienced by the family, and the managing strategies used or not used. The type of event may, in fact, be highly correlated with the family's ability or inability to manage stress or recover from crisis. Certainly, the type called "ambiguous stressor events" has been identified (e.g., Boss, 1987) as a major predictor of family stress that is difficult to resolve.

Normal Developmental Stressor Events

The classification of stressor events in the left-hand column of Figure 2.5 are the types of stressors that usually are *predictable* because they are part of everyday life and of the normal human developmental process. Birth, death, an adolescent leaving home, a young adult getting married, and older parents retiring are usually expected events during the course of family life. They are considered normal stressor events.

Although expected and normal, these events still have the potential to change a family's stress level (to higher or lower) because they disturb the status quo. But such events lead to crisis only if the family does not adapt to the changes brought about by the normal life events.

For example, retirement causes a crisis in an older, traditional family when the husband and wife continue to interact as if he still had a full-time job. To avoid conflict and dissatisfaction in the family, he may have to take on a new role, such as sharing the household duties with his wife, and she may have to make adjustments in her activities to adapt to his increased presence at home. With many normative developmental events, a family must change its boundary, that is, its

INTERNAL:
Events that begin from someone inside the family, such as getting drunk, suicide, or running for election.

EXTERNAL:
Events that begin from someone or something outside the family, such as earthquakes, terrorism, the inflation rate, or cultural attitudes toward women and minorities.

NORMATIVE:
Events that are expected over the family life cycle, such as birth, launching an adolescent, marriage, aging, or death.

NON-NORMATIVE:
Events that are unexpected, such as winning a lottery, getting a divorce, dying young, war, or being taken hostage. Often but not always disastrous.

AMBIGUOUS:
You can't get the facts surrounding the event. It's so unclear that you're not even sure that it's happening to you and your family.

NON-AMBIGUOUS:
Clear facts are available about the event: what is happening, when, how how long, and to whom.

VOLITIONAL:
Events that are wanted and sought out, such as a freely chosen job change, a college entrance, or a wanted pregnancy.

NON-VOLITIONAL:
Events that are not sought out but just happen, such as being laid off or the sudden loss of someone loved.

CHRONIC:
A situation that has long duration, such as diabetes, chemical addiction, or racial discrimination.

ACUTE:
An event that lasts a short time but is severe, such as breaking a limb, losing a job, or flunking a test.

CUMULATIVE:
Events that pile up, one right after the other, so that there is no resolution before the next one occurs. A dangerous situation in most cases.

ISOLATED:
An event that occurs alone, at least with no other events apparent at that time. It can be pinpointed easily.

Figure 2.5:   Classification of Stressor Events

perception of who is in and who is out, at every transition point. I define normative stressor events in terms of family boundary changes across the family life cycle; with each event the family either loses or gains a member so that its boundary is disturbed. For example, at retirement, the worker is back inside the family boundaries at a higher level of physical presence than before. Normal changes in family membership bear a *potential* for change—up or down—in the family's stress level. When the physical presence of family members increases or diminishes, there may be a ripple effect that causes stress levels to go up or down in marital relations, work relations, and personal health status. Such changes may affect the entire family system.

I propose, therefore, that as family boundaries change across the life cycle due to normal maturation, the family will experience increased levels of stress at each transition point, at least until the process of reorganization is accomplished after each addition or loss of a family member (Boss, 1980a, 1980b, 1987).

We now have evidence in family research that husbands and wives experience the same normative event differently, but if even one member of the family shows symptoms of stress, then the entire family system is pressured, according to systems theory. One person simply manifests the stress for the whole family. Such persons are often scapegoats—or saviors—for their family systems, a stressful position in either case. Indeed, both scapegoats and family saviors are sitting in the family hot seat.

Unexpected (Nonnormative) Stressor Events

Nonnormative stressor events (see Figure 2.5) are the kind that initially attracted family stress theorists such as Reuben Hill over four decades ago. They are unexpected (nonnormative) events and the result of some unique situation that could not be predicted and is not likely to be repeated. As a result, such events are usually highly stressful.

Negative examples of unpredictable and one-time events are disasters and catastrophes, such as the *Challenger* space shuttle explosion in 1986, wars, the Chernobyl nuclear disaster in Russia, earthquakes, volcano eruptions, tornadoes, fires, and floods.

Unexpected events that are *not* disastrous also may be stressful for families. Examples are finding lost relatives or getting unexpected job offers or promotions. Such events are positive, but they create a change or disturbance in the family's routine and, thus, contain a potential for raising the family's level of stress.

Ambiguous Stressor Events

Ambiguity is created when you cannot get the facts about the event; when the event is so unclear that you are not even sure that it's happening to you and the family. For example, your daughter talks about leaving home as soon as she finds a job, but, so far, her job seeking has not been successful; a family member has been diagnosed as dying, but because the illness is in remission, you wonder whether the doctor was wrong; or the company for which you work reports large losses and you don't know what the effect will be on your job. An earthquake may be classified as an ambiguous event if, as in California today, scientists predict that one is coming but cannot tell when or where or how severe it will be. (Were the facts more precise, more people might move to safer areas.) An ambiguous event is more difficult to deal with than a clear-cut event. It is like living with a sleeping giant; you are never quite sure when the trouble will come. More is said about this kind of stressor event in Chapter 4.

Nonambiguous Stressor Events

When clear facts are available about an event—what is happening, when, for how long, and to whom—a family is in a better position. There is no question then about *what* is happening to them, what the prognosis is, and what will help to lessen their stress. If the event, such as a hurricane, cannot be changed, they are at least clear about the duration of the storm, its logical progression, and what they must do to protect themselves.

Volitional Stressor Events

Volitional events are those that a family controls and makes happen. Making a move willingly or planning a pregnancy, for example, are volitional stressor events. Thus volitional family stressor events are classified by the degree of choice and control in the hands of family members and the system as a whole. Examples of volitional stressor events are a *wanted* marriage, a *wanted* divorce, and a deadline your family *has chosen* to meet. Some families choose to spend vacations riding a raft through the white water of the Colorado River or climbing mountains; and they enjoy playing rough games of touch football. Typically, in our culture, volitional stressor events are associated with lower degrees of family stress because the events are purposefully selected. The family remains in control of its destiny. Stories about some immigrant families, such as Lee Iacocca's and the Kennedys', reflect a constant seeking for challenge and high stress situations. The problem, however, is that not all members of a family may enjoy a high degree of stress all the time. Not everyone may be an adventurer or like competition. There may be a shy person in a family devoted to public service. When we work with families, we have to be sure that *all* family members want an event before the event can validly be classified as volitional for the entire family.

Nonvolitional Stressor Events

Nonvolitional events are those events that are thrust upon a family. They originate in the *outside* context and are not a result of action by anyone inside the family. The key point is that *the family has no control over the occurrence*. Examples of nonvolitional family stressor events are the family breadwinners being laid off from their jobs or a family member being robbed. Disastrous events that are called "acts of God," such as volcanic eruption or earthquakes, are also categorized as nonvolitional. However, even human-made disasters, such as the nuclear holocausts in Hiroshima and Nagasaki in 1945, can, from the Japanese people's perspective at least, be classified as nonvolitional; there was no knowledge of the nature of the bombs before they were dropped.

Chronic Stressor Situation

A chronic stressor is defined as a situation (as opposed to event) of disturbed equilibrium that persists over a long period of time. The situation is difficult to change. That is, the stressor is persistent. This ongoing stressor may be an illness (e.g., alcoholism or Alzheimer's disease), an economic situation (e.g., poverty or wealth), or a social condition (e.g., gender or racial discrimination). Other examples of chronic stressors are living near a constant danger (e.g., Love Canal, Mount St. Helens) or noise producer (e.g., an airport) and living in a constantly noisy atmosphere (e.g., some college dormitories). The key point is that a chronic stressor is a long-term situation rather than a one-time event.

Chronic stressors have special characteristics that affect the degree of stress experienced in a family. The following questions define the characteristics:

(1) Is there *ambiguity* rather than *predictability* in the event or situation; that is, is there uncertainty regarding facts about the onset, development, and conclusion of the event? The chronic stressor of Parkinson's disease, for example, has more predictability (due to a known medication) than does the chronic illness of Alzheimer's disease (about which little is known to date).

(2) What is the *context* in which the chronic stressor event develops; that is, is the stressful event a result of the *larger context* (e.g., inflation, living near an active volcano, or the closing of a factory) or the result of an

individual action (e.g., a lifetime of smoking that caused a persistent illness)?

(3) What is the *visibility* or *nonvisibility* of the situation? Some chronic stressors, such as diabetes or heart disease, are not physically noticeable, whereas others, such as severe retardation or loss of limb, are immediately apparent to the outsider as well as to family members.

Each of these characteristics may affect the family's perception of the event that, in turn, will determine the degree of stress the family will experience; thus we must collect answers to foregoing questions when we work with chronically stressed families.

A Note on the Difficulties of Assessing Chronic Stressor Situations

Even more than with short-term events, the subtle characteristics of chronic stressor situations call for special consideration in research methodology, clinical diagnosis, and assessment of family stress. Instruments must have the capacity to measure perceptual variables that are influenced by the *duration* and *ambiguity* of long-term stressor situations. Tests and measuring instruments must be sensitive to the possibility of the family's denying what is happening to them. For example, the family may totally deny the existence of a persisting illness in its member. We find such denial with many chronic illnesses, for example alcoholism, drug addiction, Alzheimer's disease, and end-stage renal disease.

Another characteristic unique to a chronic stressor situation influences research as well as therapeutic assessment. It is that the family's perception of the situation may *change* over the family life cycle. According to Lynn Wikler (1981), a social work researcher, chronic stressors, such as severe retardation, become "recycled" at each juncture of the life span when a developmental step would normally occur in the affected person. For example, when a retarded child reaches the age of high school graduation and cannot be graduated and launched as normal children are, the family is newly reminded of the hopelessness of the child's situation. Because of their normal expectations, the family's chronic stress may be raised to a higher level at each developmental point. A chronic stressor event is an added complication when it overlaps the normal stressor events of developmental family life transitions that occur naturally over the life span. The caregiver and the family may not be able to absorb the pileup of both the stressor situation (e.g., a chronically ill family member) *plus* normal stressor events (e.g., an aged parent's dying and an adolescent's leaving home), which happen during the same period. Managing all these changes becomes too much. We can predict, therefore, that families will be highly stressed whenever a normal developmental transition overlaps a chronic family stressor situation, even though the family manages the illness before and after that transition point reasonably well.

To summarize, a chronic stressor should be defined as a stressful situation (rather than an event) that is characterized by (a) *long duration*, (b) *the probability of pileup with other events, especially normal developmental transitions*, and (c) *the potential of high ambiguity in its origin (etiology), progression, and conclusion*. (More is said about ambiguity in Chapter 4.)

Acute Stressor Events

Acute stressor events are events that happen suddenly and last only a short time. The period of time they last are usually predictable. Examples are a child's breaking a leg and then having to wear a cast for six weeks or a family member undergoing emergency surgery and then having to stay home from work for six weeks to recuperate.

The major distinction between a chronic and acute stressor event is that the latter happens suddenly and then is over. The duration of the acute stressor event is short and reasonably predictable. We know what we have to deal with more than we do with chronic events.

Isolated Stressor Events

Isolated stressor events are *single* events that occur at a time when nothing else is disturbing the family status quo. This single event can then be pinpointed as *the* event that is causing the disturbance.

Accumulation of Stressor Events

The accumulation of stressor events is a phenomenon in which several stressor events or situations occur *at the same time or in quick sequence*, thus compounding the degree of pressure on the family. The idea of accumulation is the basis of the frequently used Holmes and Rahe (1967) Schedule of Recent Events, which quantifies self-reported stress pileup for *individuals*, and the Family Inventory of Life Events and Changes Scale, developed by McCubbin, Patterson, and Wilson

(1981), which quantifies stress pileup as reported by a family member. The concept of stress pileup is important because it is the accumulation of several stressor events rather than the nature of one isolated event that determines a family's level of stress, its subsequent vulnerability to crisis, or its ability to recover from a particular crisis. An event rarely happens to a family in total isolation; at least, normal developmental changes are always taking place as family members are born, mature, grow older, and die. Indeed, families are *always* changing for developmental reasons, if no other. Perfect equilibrium is never achieved, nor should it be.

THE MEANING OF THE STRESSFUL EVENT
TO THE FAMILY

The meaning of a stressful event for a family is also called the family's perception or appraisal, definition, or assessment of the event. I prefer the term *perception* because it embodies both cognitive and affective (feeling) processes. The family's perception of the event is important in explaining *why*, given the same event, some families can manage the resulting stress whereas others go into crisis. *How* the family perceives the event or situation that is happening to them is critical in determining the degree of stress felt by the family and the outcome, that is, crisis or coping. What seems stressful to one family may not be stressful to others. How the family sees an event also determines how they cope or what alternative (if any) they see for resolving the problem. Some families endure; some overcome. The big question is *why*.

When individual perceptions in a family are congruent, we have a collective perception. Everyone in the family sees the event and the alternatives for coping with it the same way. At first we might think that such congruence is ideal, but too often in clinics we see families that share only a distortion of reality. In such cases, all members of the family have the same unrealistic view of the event.

An example of such a family was reported by family therapist-researcher Lynn Wikler (Pollner & McDonald-Wikler, 1985; Wikler, 1981), of the University of Wisconsin. The family (as a whole) perceived their retarded child as normal for an extended period of time despite clear evidence to the contrary from doctors and teachers. It was as if the whole family had implicitly agreed to believe something else, and they did. They talked to the retarded child as if he were normal; they ignored his feeble behavior; and, as a unit, they interacted as if he were normal. The child suffered increasingly from the family's delusion, a phenomenon that Wikler labeled "folie à famille" (*folie* is French for "delusion"). This denial of reality by the family put them on the path to trouble.

Delusional systems can be maintained only until some change occurs, for example, when a retarded child is removed from a regular class and placed in special education, or the child's peers graduate and go on to high school and college, or the child is now an adult but cannot function independently. Change is inevitable in family systems if for no other reason than that people mature and grow older. Family systems that share a distortion of reality are very fragile. Unfortunately, the tragedy is that some delusional families can go on for generations before their denial of reality is broken. Incest, for example, thrives in families only under delusional conditions.

SOME FAMILY DISTORTIONS OF REALITY

Mom is not really alcoholic; she just has a bad back and needs to stay in bed a lot.

Women in the family are meant to serve the men. At holiday dinners, the men are served first; then the women sit down and eat while the men go into the living room.

We are a powerless family. Other families have power, but we don't. We just flow with the wind and take what life dishes out to us since we can't do much to change things anyhow. Only the big shots have power.

These examples support the assumption that there is a "family perception of the event." As in any system, especially a human one, the whole is greater than the sum of its parts; the family's definition of reality is powerful and even may supersede the meaning that individual family members give to the same event. However, when even one family member begins to see things differently from the collective, then change is on its way for all that family.

In subsequent chapters, I discuss three factors that heavily influence how a family perceives or assesses a stressor event. They are (a) boundary ambiguity, (b) denial, and (c) the family's value orientation. Because of their importance and their newness to the family stress literature, each is discussed in depth.

FAMILY STRESS

Family stress is pressure on the family. It is a disturbance of the family's steady state, that is, the system is upset, pressured, disturbed, and not at rest. Family stress, therefore, is *change* in the family's equilibrium. This is not necessarily bad. It becomes problematic when the degree of stress (pressure or change) in the family system reaches a level (either too low or too high) at which family members become dissatisfied or show symptoms of disturbance. If even one family member is dissatisfied or manifests physical or emotional symptoms, then the *degree of family stress* is not optimal for that family. They are in trouble.

If we use an engineering metaphor, we can liken family stress to a force pressing, pushing, or pulling on the family structure. Although this force can originate either inside or outside the family system, it is the pressure *inside* the family system that indicates the level of stress. An engineer checking a bridge for degree of stress looks for an increase in weight exerted on the bridge; a physician checking an individual's health looks for an increase in blood pressure; but a family therapist or researcher assessing *family stress* looks for (a) lowered performance in the family's usual routines and tasks and (b) the occurrence of physical or emotional symptoms in individual family members. On a bridge, if just one pillar in the structure is weak, then the whole bridge is being strained. The same is true for families. Lowered performance in family roles and psychosomatic symptoms signal danger when the level of stress on a family's structure increases.

Keep in mind that family stress does not have to end in trouble. A high-tension bridge, for example, is intact and functional despite the tension; and so some high-tension families also remain solid and functional. Like the bridge, high-tension families must have flexibility and "sway" in their structure if they are to avoid collapse, however. In highly stressed but functional families, there must be flexibility in family rules, roles, and problem-solving skills. They must be able to change constantly to adapt to the situation at hand, and there must be a continuing negotiation between the family's *pressures* and *supports*. Such flexible family systems can withstand a lot of pressure, because not only do they have support and strength behind them but they have the ability to sway under pressure as well. Keep the bridge metaphor in mind to understand family tension better.

It is likely that some families simply enjoy and tolerate more stress than others. This characteristic also points to the importance of the family's perception or appraisal of a stressor event or situation. It may be that some families get bored without a constant string of stressful events to excite them or without the challenge of constant problems to solve. Such families actually may seek out new stressors. They *like* to move often; they travel often; they seek out competition; they like a challenge. They may engage in all sorts of stressful activities without negative effects.

In sum, family stress is a neutral construct. It is neither negative nor positive. It simply means pressure on the family. The degree of stress that results in the family and the appearance of deleterious or positive effects depend a great deal on the family's perception and appraisal of the situation. By itself, family stress is neither negative or positive. It simply means change, a disturbed equilibrium in the family system.

FAMILY CRISIS

Family stress sometimes results in crisis (see Figure 2.6). A family crisis is (a) a disturbance in the equilibrium that is so overwhelming, (b) a pressure that is so severe, or (c) a change that is so acute that the family system is blocked, immobilized, and incapacitated. At least for a time, the family does not function. Family boundaries are no longer maintained, customary roles and tasks are no longer performed, and family members can no longer function at optimal levels, physically or psychologically.

The following case from my own family illustrates my point:

It was the summer of 1955, the summer before the Salk polio vaccine was discovered. Polio was rampant and many of the young were stricken. Eddie was young and strong and the predicted star of the freshman football team. But tragedy struck. He played football one Friday, and he was buried the next. The football squad carried his coffin at the funeral, and the whole school and community were in shock. The family was immobilized. Friends and people from the community had to come into the home with food. They had to help chauffeur, plan the funeral, and fill in for family members at work and at school. Eddie's family could not perform tasks and chores in the usual way. Each member withdrew into her or his own private grief. The family rule of "we take care of ourselves" gave way and friends and neighbors took over to help. The family system was in crisis. It was immobilized.

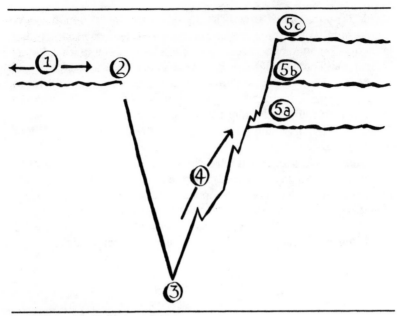

Figure 2.6:   The Turning Point in Family Crisis

SOURCE: Adapted from Hill (1949) and Koos (1946).

NOTE: (1) = level of family functioning before event occurred; (2) = event occurs; (3) = "hitting bottom"; (4) = the turning point: period of recovery; (5) = level of reorganization: (a) below previous level of functioning; (b) equal to previous level of functioning; (c) higher than previous level of functioning.

When a family is in crisis, it means, continuing the engineering metaphor, that the bridge has collapsed. The structure has broken down and is no longer functional, it cannot support people or maintain boundaries. Specific indicators of family crisis are (a) inability of family members to perform usual roles and tasks, (b) inability to make decisions and solve problems, (c) inability to care for each other in the usual way, and (d) focus shifting from family to individual survival. Family members no longer take care of each other. They may not even be able to take care of themselves for a time. As in the preceding case study, friends and neighbors may have to shore up the family for a while.

Based on these indicators, we see in the case study (a) the inability of parents to take care of themselves, their children, their work, or their business; (b) the inability of family members to make decisions or to solve problems (e.g., about the funeral, money, or work); (c) and the inability of family members to function, so that outsiders are temporarily needed to come in and perform usual family roles and tasks.

Many families avoid crisis by holding the degree of stress to a tolerable level, a process called coping, adapting, management, or problem solving (see Chapter 3). Nor have all families in crisis had long-term stress; they may have been doing well until a disaster struck. The strongest of families will fall into momentary crisis when an accident takes away a limb, when an earthquake swallows a house, or when a loved one suddenly dies.

The Turning Point:
Family Recovery After Crisis

Crisis is painful and may debilitate the family. The length of the debilitation may vary from hours to years. Family crisis does not mean that the family is immobilized forever; it can "hit bottom," begin the recovery process, and repair itself (see Figure 2.6 for illustration). This ability to recover marks the major difference between a mechanical system (the bridge) and an organic system (the family). A family system has the potential to grow and learn from a crisis, whereas a bridge does not. For human systems, therefore, crisis may be simply a turning point, not an end-point. This important difference provides a very hopeful note for families in crisis.

After the funeral, Eddie's family slowly and painfully began recovering. They began to work again and to eat, and even, occasionally, to find something to smile at. Routines returned. Help from the outside was needed less and less. The parents even went to talk with others who had lost children so suddenly. A year later, family members all helped the March of Dimes raise funds for further research on polio. The family system was no longer in crisis. After hitting bottom, it was on the way to a new organization, one without Eddie except in memory. Some stress from that event of loss will always be with the family but it is clear that the family is no longer immobilized. The crisis is over.

Recovery

When the *ratio* between the *family system's support* and the *pressure* on it shifts so that the pressure lowers and the supports become stronger, recovery is taking place. Turning points result from (a) a change in the stressor event, (b) a change in the availability of resources for coping, or (c) a change in the family's *perception* of both factors. In case of incurable illness or where the pressure of the event cannot be lessened, we can ease the stress level with factors (b) and (c). If, however, the family's resources cannot be increased, then we can intervene with (c) only, changing the family's perception of what is happening to them.

The Difference Between Stress and Crisis

To summarize the discussion on stress and crisis, I want to reemphasize that the terms *stress* and *crisis* cannot be used interchangeably. Whereas family stress is a state of *disturbed equilibrium*, family crisis is a point of *acute disequilibrium*. Family stress, therefore, is a *continuous* variable (degrees of stress), whereas family crisis is a *categorical* variable (a family either is in crisis or it is not; see Figures 2.4 and 2.6). In crisis, the family system either holds or it does not. Like a bridge that collapses, a family crisis is determined by the point at which the family structure can no longer perform its intended functions. In a family, however, in addition to the pressures that outweigh the family supports, the family's perception and appraisal of what is happening influences the point at which crisis occurs.

Some families reach a turning point after crisis by redefining the events that have been stressing them, or they redefine their existing strengths, resources, and supports. Even if nothing else changes, families may have changed their perception of what was happening to them or what resources and supports they had to cope with. Clinicians call this process "reframing." Such a change in perception can alter the ratio of family pressure to family support and thereby precipitate a "turning point," the beginning of recovery for a family in crisis. This is important in crises when the event of loss, as in Eddie's family, cannot be changed. We cannot change the event, so we change our perception of it. In other crises, we might change the event (e.g., by finding a cure for a disease), or we can increase our emotional supports (e.g., joining a support group).

We can see in Figure 2.6 that crisis does not have to permanently break up the family system. It may only temporarily immobilize the family and then, after the turning point, lead to a different level of functioning than the family experienced before their stress level escalated to the point of crisis. Many family systems become stronger than they were originally after they have experienced and recovered from crisis.

FAMILY STRAIN (BURNOUT)

Family strain can be likened to a bridge shaking but not yet collapsing. The structure is still functional—at least minimally—but it is bent out of shape, creaking, and it shakes under pressure. Strain results from a mismatch at the point where pressures occur and the supports are grounded. In a family system, that means supports (resources and strengths) may exist but they are not where they are most needed. For example, the family may have plenty of money (a resource), but the resources needed to meet the pressures they are facing at the moment (e.g., illness of an elderly parent, moving, or a hyperactive child) are more psychological than monetary. More often, we see the opposite: psychologically strong families who are economically poor. Such a mismatch causes family strain. When a family has a mismatch between the location of their strengths and pressures, it may function shakily, that is minimally, and with great difficulty.

The danger of strain for a family is that if their structure begins to change at some time (and that is quite likely just because children grow up and parents grow older), the existing mismatch limits the family's degree of tolerance to adapt to stress. A strained family is brittle. Thus in an already strained family, the chance for total collapse (crisis) is high when stress is added. The family becomes what we call "highly vulnerable."

It may be more critical, then, to avoid the mismatch of strain than it is to avoid stressor events. We need to know how much pressure we can handle; there are times when we can handle more pressure than at other times. The family that is not strained can more easily manage and cope with everyday stressor events because resources can easily be directed to match pressures where they occur. In addition, although the mismatch that defines family strain does not always depend on the accumulation of stressor events, the mismatch is more likely to occur when events pile up persistently and exert increasing pressure at different points of the family structure, thus aggravating the dangerous mismatch.

For professionals working with families, the identification of vulnerable families may be easier if they look for this *mismatch* between stressors and strengths, between pressures and supports, to tell which families are fragile and which are strong. Some families can handle a lot of pressure; others cannot. Strain, more than stress or crisis, may be a distinguishing variable in identifying vulnerable families.

POINTS TO REMEMBER

(1) Families are not isolated systems. They deal with stress within two contexts. The external context is made up of those elements over which a family has no control. The internal context is made up of those elements that a family is able to control.

(2) Elements of the external context of family stress are culture, history, economics, development (maturation), and the genetic inheritance that interplays with environment.

(3) Elements of the internal context of family stress are the family's structure, its psychological defenses, and its philosophical beliefs.

(4) The basic stress equation, ABC-X, was conceived by Reuben Hill.

A = stressor event
B = family resources
C = perception of event, and
X = outcome: the resulting degree of stress (high = strained, low = managed) or crisis. Degree of stress is a continuous variable; crisis is a categorical variable.

A linear equation for understanding family stress is no longer valid, but elements remain useful.

(5) The family's perception of the event (C) is the least studied and the most important part of the stress equation.

(6) Family stress, crisis, and strain are different terms and cannot be used synonymously. Family stress means *change in the equilibrium* of the family system. It may be a change the family enjoys and seeks out, or it may be a change they would prefer to avoid. In either case, family stress does not necessarily lead to crisis.

(7) Family crisis is brought about by such severe stress that the family cannot function; they are immobilized. When crisis happens, the family "hits bottom" and then, one hopes, reaches a "turning point." This is the point at which the recovery process begins. The family can end up even stronger than before the crisis occurred.

FURTHER READING

Akutagawa, R. (1952). *Rashomon and other stories* (T. Kojima, Trans.). Tokyo: Charles E. Tuttle.

Aldous, J. (1978). *Family careers: Developmental change in family.* New York: John Wiley.

Cobb, S. (1974). A model for life events and their consequences. In B. S. Dohrenwend & B. P. Dohrenwend (Eds.), *Stressful life events: Their nature and effects.* New York: John Wiley.

Figley, C. R., & McCubbin, H. I. (1983). *Stress and the family: Vol. 2. Coping with catastrophe.* New York: Brunner/Mazel.

Golan, N. (1975). Wife to widow to woman: A process of role transition. *Social Work, 20,* 396-374.

Golan, N. (1978). *Treatment in crisis situations.* New York: Free Press.

Gonzalez, S., & Reiss, D. (1981). *Families and chronic illness: Technical difficulties in assessing adjustment.* Paper presented at the annual meeting of the National Council on Family Relations, Theory Construction Workshop, Milwaukee.

Holmes, T. H., & Rahe, R. H. (1967, September). The social readjustment rating scale. *Journal of Psychosomatic Research, 11,* 213-218.

Leik, R. K., Leik, S. A., Ekker, K., & Gifford, G. A. (1982, February). *Under the threat of Mt. St. Helens: A study of chronic family stress.* Final report for Federal Emergency Management Agency, Office of Prevention, National Institute of Mental Health, Washington, DC.

McCubbin, H. I., & Boss, P. G. (Eds.). (1980). Family stress, coping and adaptation [Special issue]. *Family Relations, 29*(4).

McCubbin, H., Dahl, B., & Hunter, E. (1976). Research on the military family: A review. In H. McCubbin, B. Dahl, & E. Hunter (Eds.), *Families in the military system.* Beverly Hills, CA: Sage.

McCubbin, H., Dahl, B., Lester, G., & Boss, P. (1975). *Coping with Separation Inventory (CSI).* San Diego, CA: Naval Health Research Center.

McCubbin, H. I., & Figley, C. R. (1983). *Stress and the family: Vol. 1. Coping with normative transitions.* New York: Brunner/Mazel.

McCubbin, H., Hunter, E., & Dahl, B. (1975, Fall). Families of prisoners of war and servicemen missing in action. *Journal of Social Issues, 31,* 95-109.

McCubbin, H., Joy, C., Cauble, B., Comeau, J., Patterson, J., & Needle, R. (1980). Family stress and coping: A decade review. *Journal of Marriage and the Family, 42*(4), 855-871.

McCubbin, H. I., & Patterson, J. M. (1981). *Systematic assessment of family stress, resources, and coping: Tools for research, education and clinical intervention.* St. Paul: University of Minnesota.

McCubbin, H., Patterson, J., & Wilson, L. (1981). *Family Inventory of Life Events and Changes (FILE): Research Instrument.* St. Paul: University of Minnesota.

McCubbin, H., Sussman, M., & Patterson, J. (Eds.). (1983a). *Advances in family stress theory and research.* New York: Haworth Press.

McCubbin, H., Sussman, M., & Patterson, J. (Eds.). (1983b). *Social stress and the family.* New York: Haworth Press.

Mederer, H., & Hill, R. (1983). Critical transitions over the family life span: Theory and research. In H. McCubbin, M. Sussman, & J. Patterson (Eds.), *Social stress and the family.* New York: Haworth Press.

Neugarten, B., & Hagestad, G. (1977). Age and the life course. In R. H. Binstock & E. Shanas (Eds.), *Handbook on aging and the social science.* New York: Van Nostrand Reinhold.

Papalia, D. E., & Olds, S. W. (1986). *Human development.* New York: McGraw-Hill.

Riegel, K. (1976, October). A manifesto for dialectical psychology. *American Psychologist, 10,* 692-693.

Riegel, K. (1979). *Foundations of dialectical psychology.* New York: Academic Press.

Russell, C. (1974, May). Transition to parenthood. *Journal of Marriage and the Family, 36,* 294-302.

Wikler, L. (1981). Chronic stresses of families of mentally retarded children. *Family Relations, 30*(2), 281-288.

CHAPTER
3

Coping,
Adapting . . . or
Is It Managing?

THE MAJOR SHIFT in family stress research during the decades of the 1970s and 1980s has been from "crisis" to "coping." In the 1970s, family social scientists for the first time became more concerned with family successes than family failures. Because families cannot escape *normal* developmental stressor events and few can avoid *unexpected* events, such as illness, accidents, or disasters, stress but not crisis is inevitable. From this new perspective, researchers studying military and corporate executive families were able to ascertain how strong families cope and survive.[1] With this knowledge, they then were able to provide information on how to strengthen vulnerable families before or after the occurrence of stressful events (e.g., father absence, war, imprisonment, missing-in-action, and frequent family moves due to job demands).

The research and theoretical models of the 1970s, therefore, shifted from a focus on family crisis to one on prevention. Knowing how severely stressed families survive can help to make all families less vulnerable to crises.

It was during this decade that a new concept called *coping* was introduced to family stress literature. At first glance, family coping appears to be the same as the construct "family resources," which was described by Reuben Hill in his ABC-X model. Coping, however, is a new dimension not found in the original ABC-X model. Indeed, coping behaviors are part of the family's resources; but coping is much more than that. In this chapter, I will first review coping from the individual psychological perspective and then wrestle with the dilemma of individual versus family coping, giving some research and clinical background for that definition. Finally, I share cautions and complexities about the use of the term coping, and suggest that the term *managing* gives more clarity to the ultimate goal for a stressed family.

COPING IN INDIVIDUAL STRESS THEORY

From a cognitive and phenomenological perspective, Richard Lazarus, a psychologist, defined coping as a cognitive activity incorporating (a) an assessment of impending harm (primary appraisal) and (b) an assessment of the consequences of any coping action (secondary appraisal; 1966, 1976). Thus the *coping process*, according to Lazarus, is the cognitive use of primary and secondary *appraisals* of what is happening, whereas *coping strategies* or behaviors are the actual *responses* to a perceived threat. *Coping behaviors* are defined by Lazarus as (a) *direct action behaviors*, an attack or escape from threat (fight or flight), which are used to change a stressed relation with one's physical or social environment, and (b) *intrapsychic forms of coping*, which are defense mechanisms (e.g., detachment or denial) used to reduce emotional arousal rather than to change the situation. Both *actions* and *thoughts* may make a person feel better even if he or she cannot change the source of the stress (Lazarus, 1976).

Although Lazarus's theoretical work is psychological in nature and directed to individual stress, it is also relevant to family stress theory. He emphasized the importance of cognition as well as the individual's psychological profile (values, beliefs, expectations, and motivations)— the same indicators that are important in family stress management. When Reuben Hill emphasized the importance of the *meaning* a stressor event had for the family, values and beliefs, expectations and motivations implicitly came to the fore in the primary and secondary appraisals of the family's threat. Given these commonalities, we merge sociological and psychological conceptualizations in order to help us understand families in stress better.

Psychologist Richard Lazarus (1966, 1976) defines *individual* coping as "(a) direct action behaviors (fight or flight) which deal with the stressor itself, and (b) palliative behaviors (actions or thoughts which make the person feel more calm)." Lazarus holds that an individual's coping behavior is organized not by emotions but by the *cognitive process* that leads to the *emotional response*. A coping behavior may be chosen for more than one purpose: (a) *to deal with the problem* generated by the stress emotion (fight or flight) and (b) *to control the*

emotion (by covering it up). For example, going to visit an older sister or
brother is coping behavior that deals with the isolation brought about
after you break up with someone you care about, and with the
depression and loneliness that arise from the loss. Deciding to reach out
to a sibling not only helps to alleviate the physical isolation but eases
one's depression as well. The decision to reach out is "fight behavior." It
may result from cognition (recognition of loss) leading to an emotional
response (sadness, loneliness, regret) that organizes the person's
behavior (calling up your sister or brother, asking if you may visit,
walking to the car, driving to his or her house, expressing how you feel,
and so on).

What I have described, however, is functional coping. Dysfunctional
coping also may take place in families. Because of learned behavior and
implicit family rules or paradigms and, most of all, because of strong
family denial systems, coping strategies in dysfunctional families appear
to be automatic and not cognitively planned. For example, a parent may
cope with job frustration by coming home and abusing the children, or a
stressed person may reach for a drink or food without even thinking (a
palliative coping behavior). A family can move to cognition and begin
the functional coping process only after its denial system is penetrated.
If the problem is one of physical or sexual abuse, a primary goal of family
treatment is to help individuals within this denying family system do
some cognitive restructuring. This is not an easy task for a family,
especially if the dysfunctional pattern of coping has been accepted for
several generations.

The job of the therapist, then, is to stimulate, mediate, or facilitate
the family's recognition of reality. It can be done by using various
approaches to therapy. First, however, the family's agreement on what
they see and feel must be challenged. This may not happen all at once.
Sometimes just one person in the family breaks through the denial
system and begins the process toward functional coping. When even
one person's reality in a family changes, the entire family never can be
the same again. The process of change has begun.

FAMILY AND INDIVIDUAL COPING:
THE NEED FOR A DIALECTICAL VIEW

Family stress theory is full of opposing elements: adaptation versus
revolution; coping versus crisis; conflict versus solidarity; independence
and self-sufficiency versus family cohesion; and, the most basic of all
opposing elements in family research, the individual versus the family.

For this reason, family researchers, therapists, and educators must incorporate dialectical thinking into their work with stressed families. Research is especially needed to verify dialectics as a reality in family life.

When we talk about family and individual coping, the question arises of whether the phenomenon of *family* coping exists or whether family coping is simply a collection of individuals who are coping. From a social-psychological and dialectical perspective, the answer is *both*. Let me explain. I have said that both individual and family coping are important, so the theoretical perspective becomes one of dialectics. Sociologist Walter Buckley (1967) identified three types of systems theory, the mechanistic, the organismic, and the dialectical. Only a worldview based on dialectical theory allows a researcher or therapist to incorporate the complexity and process dimensions of family stress and coping. Family therapists such as Maurizio Andolfi, Marilyn Mason, Helm Stierlin, Carl Whitaker, and even I use a dialectical perspective of systems theory; researchers, however, only recently have begun to consider this perspective feasible for the study of families in stress.

The dialectical worldview stems from the work of Aristotle, an early Greek philosopher, who said that the elements of a universe *are held together by opposition*. Dialectics, therefore, is a philosophy based on the process of movement, development, and interaction. (This implies change.) The process depends upon elements in opposition, such as destruction, emergence, and alteration, which are the bases for change. In the early 1800s, this same philosophy became the basis for the German philosopher Georg Wilhelm Friedrich Hegel's premise of progressive development. He said that from every *thesis* there evolves an *antithesis*, and these two result in the development of *synthesis* (unified whole) that, in turn, reacts on the original thesis. The process goes on and on.

Hegel's notion of thesis and antithesis was introduced to the field of psychology by Erik Erikson in 1950. He described individuals and society or parents and children as contradictions to each other. Klaus Riegel, a developmental psychologist, carried the case for the dialectical perspective even further into American psychological theory by noting the conflicting development of individuals in four areas: the biological, the psychological, the physical, and the cultural. For example, the psychological development of adolescents may not always be in harmony with their physical development; if a family moves to a new culture during this time, the conflicting development for an adolescent will be compounded.

This idea fits families. For example, parents want their children to leave home, but they also want them to stay and to be loyal to them. Children both want to leave home and be different and to stay, especially if the home is comfortable. Out of this push and pull there comes, ideally, a synthesis for both parents and offspring. The adult children remain a part of the family but in a *new* way; rules and boundaries are changed and even rituals.

FAMILY COPING DEFINED

From the dialectical perspective, the definition of family coping in this chapter includes both *individual* and *group* indicators and aspects of both adaptation and maladaptation. The cognitive appraisal of a stressful situation or event, the emotional reaction to it, and the behavioral responses to both the appraisal and the emotion all happen within the individual family member, albeit within a systems context.

From the family therapy perspective, I also add the assumption that individuals are highly influenced by their past and present systems. Newlyweds bring with them rules of decision making and problem solving learned in their families of origin, even when they dislike these rules and would like to leave them behind.

Although family coping was defined by McCubbin et al. (1980) as the group's management of a stressful event or situation, I maintain that a family as a group is *not* coping functionally if even *one* member manifests distress symptoms. However much the family as a whole may look calm and "as if" it is managing the effects of a particular stressor event, closer examination often shows that, for example, the mother is depressed, an adolescent has psychosomatic problems, or the father's blood pressure is dangerously high; in some families everyone retreats behind closed doors when an argument gets too hot; in others, someone acts out mischievously to heat up family life when it is boring and cool. Both the individual and the family system as a whole are involved in the coping process. Thus the exploration of *individual* as well as *group* indicators is essential to assess family coping. In this regard, I am cautious about the use of the concepts of coping, adaptation, and adjustment if the implicit value is family peace over family conflict.

I therefore define family coping to mean *the management of a stressful event or situation by the family as a unit with no detrimental effects on any individual in that family. Family coping is the cognitive, affective, and behavioral process by which individuals and their family system as a whole manage rather than eradicate stressful events or situations.*

Initially, one person or the family as a whole may accidentally hit upon the behaviors that ease the problem. Or they may decide to take a certain course of action that has proved effective by trial and error or by rational decision making. In any event, once the family finds a coping behavior that works for a particular event, that behavior very likely becomes a part of that family's repertoire as a *coping, problem-solving, or management* strategy.

DEDUCTIVE EVIDENCE FOR THIS SOCIAL-PSYCHOLOGICAL DEFINITION OF FAMILY COPING

The social-psychological definition of family coping just presented is deductively based on the series of poststressor studies that were carried out during the 1970s at the Center for Prisoner of War Studies in San Diego. These studies centered on coping *after* the stressor event of family separation, or father absence, in most cases due to military service in Vietnam or job responsibilities in a corporation (Boss, 1975a, 1975b, 1977, 1980b; Boss, McCubbin, & Lester, 1979; Hunter, 1983; McCubbin, 1979).

Findings from these studies and from McCubbin, Patterson, and Wilson (1981), Boss (1983a), and LaVee, McCubbin, and Patterson (1985) indicate that certain coping behavior patterns were constant across *all* samples: (a) *establishing independence and self-sufficiency* by the remaining parent, and (b) *maintaining family integrity* (in all populations except the corporate executive families).

It appears from this series of investigations that coping and problem-solving strategies focus on self-development as well as on the integration of the family as a system. This finding is consistent with Buckley's systems theory (1967) and, most significant, with the findings of early family stress researchers (Angell, 1936/1965; Hill, 1949), which suggests that the families that cope best with stress *are strong as a unit as well as in individual members.*

The surfacing of these two major coping strategies (establishing independence/self-sufficiency and maintaining family integrity/stability) indicate the importance of both individual (psychological) and group (sociological) variables in the research and treatment of families in stress. In earlier sociological models (Burr, 1973), individual psychological variables were not made explicit; and in psychological research, family and contextual variables have not been apparent. I maintain that both are essential.

From this research on family stress, it appears that a dialectical balance between individual and family variables provides the most valid theoretical base for a deeper understanding of the family coping or stress management process. This body of research also indicates that the coping strategies used by families fall into the same categories as those outlined by Lazarus for individual coping: (a) direct action behavior (i.e., learning new skills, advancing a professional career); (b) intrapsychic forms of coping (i.e., never showing fear, believing that life would not be any better if the absent spouse were present); and (c) behavior that controls the emotion generated by the stressor event (i.e., professional counseling, keeping a diary or journal, drinking alcohol, and so on). The fact that findings from recent family coping research are compatible with those of Angell's early research on families of the depression of 1929, Hill's studies of World War II families, as well as Lazarus' individual coping research indicates that we are indeed moving in the right direction in this relatively new area of inquiry.

THE POSSIBILITY OF
"INHERITED" COPING STRATEGIES

Family coping strategies are not inherited but the existence of family rules and patterns of coping can be passed on from generation to generation. This sequence frequently is seen by clinicians, especially those who treat abusive family systems. In the latter, families pass down rules that permit such behaviors as physical aggression and submission. For example, when Dad feels down, he may have learned (albeit wrongly) from watching his father that he can hit Mom and the kids. Although such behavior directed at family members is dysfunctional, unfortunately dysfunctional coping patterns (e.g., violence and aggression) as well as their counterpart (passivity) continue to be transmitted across the generations. It is this transmission that needs to be interrupted if a family is to change (see also Gelles & Cornell, 1986).

A CAUTION ABOUT COPING

Family invulnerability and strength is more than just "taking it on the chin" and surviving under pressure; it also includes the options of rebellion and change. Thus, I conclude, the word *coping* should be used with caution. Too often the term is used in family stress theory to represent a homeostatic status quo model of the family (i.e., no change) rather than the active managing of stress that leads to a new level of organization. This regression toward the status quo has been called to the attention of family stress researchers by ethnic, minority, and feminist scholars and theorists, but to date no family stress researcher has made this caution explicit. I do that here.

Too often in family stress theory, the meaning given to the term coping has not allowed for the possibility of change, either through evolution or revolution. In architecture, for example, *to cope* means to bend, to meet pressure by curving or bending, as an arch or vault in the ceiling. Coping in families has also implied bending and shoring up pressure points rather than challenging the cause of the pressure. *Family coping* has been used as a rule to mean making things work in the face of difficulty or to adopt a stoical attitude instead of to rebel or change. I am, therefore, cautious about the value of the meanings we have given to the concept of coping. It may not always be good to cope, in the general usage of the term in family stress theory.

Often I see families in therapy who have worked too hard at being strong and "keeping an even keel" in the face of what is happening to them. They "tough it out" when most other families would give up or rebel. They maintain the status quo at all costs. And the costs mount up.

Sometimes it may be better for a family to give up, to let go, *to fail to cope* even if that precipitates crisis. At least after crisis the family can reorganize into a new system with new rules. It is better, for example, for a teenager to revolt and leave home than to continue to try to cope with a battering or incestuous parent. The crisis caused by leaving may lead to change, which may be what that family needs. In such cases, it is better if the family system explodes, runs amuck, falls apart, hits bottom, and goes into crisis. This, at least, would allow for reorganization of family boundaries and rules. Such a family can survive, but first it has to come apart so that change and reorganization are possible. Change is what is needed in incestuous and violent families, *not* coping (in its usual family stress meaning) and adaptation.

Sudden fluctuations or revolutionary changes in the family system are not always bad. Changes may lead to a higher level of functioning for the family than was possible before the crisis. As with a shaking bridge, slowing the speed of traffic or rerouting may be only temporary solutions. There comes a time when the only thing left to do is to take down the old bridge and build a new one. The same is true for families. Sometimes we must give up on the old and build anew. The process is painful; it does not necessarily require divorce or an exiting of family members. What it does require, however, is new boundaries and rules in the family system. The original family members can survive restructuring if they are willing and, perhaps, coached to make changes. It alarms me that much of the family literature appears to assume that calm, serenity, orderliness, and stability are the desired ends for family life. The latter exists best in a context of "moving the equilibrium" over time. That means *discontinuous* change through the life cycle and the presence of conflict as part of the process. If we limit ourselves to valuing only adapting (as opposed to conflict and change), then we are limiting families to a perspective that promotes "fitting in" and adjusting to whomever or whatever is causing stress in families. For example, family members learn to "walk on eggs" not to disturb an angry or fragile parent. Yet that parent could be ill and in need of treatment (in cases of alcoholism or bipolar depression) or just bad-tempered and spoiled. In either case, the family members have implicitly agreed to adapt to this person's behavior rather than to ask for change or seek help for change.

When change is presented as negative and *lack* of change as positive, we are in danger of applauding families for adaptations that are restrictive. If a family appears peaceful, at least in public, it may be at the expense of the physical and psychological symptoms of high stress shown by individual family members.

Herein lies my caution. Coping (i.e., adapting, suppressing, or giving in) at all costs moves us alarmingly close to passive acceptance of the status quo. A wife who puts up with abuse and then prides herself on being strong enough to take it is playing the martyr and coping stoically. When a child is diagnosed as having a malignant tumor and the parents resign themselves to accepting the child's illness as God's will rather than following the treatment prescribed by the medical team, they are coping passively. Neither example is life-enhancing.

Professionals working with stressed families must be open to the fact that being accepting or stoic may be a way for families to cope and adapt to stressful events but that sometimes it may be better for change to occur; for family rules to be broken; for boundaries to change; and for revolution and conflict to occur.

Even though it looks like failure when a family fails to cope, the failure itself can be positive. A family that no longer tries to adapt to stress and falls into crisis may recover to a level of functioning even higher than the one they had before the crisis. They go through what Paul Watzlawick (Watzlawick, Weakland, & Fisch, 1974) calls a "second-order change," which represents a "shift in gears" for the family system. That means because its rules for interaction have changed, the family has actually changed. Addictions have been treated; intergenerational boundaries have been clarified; secrets have been aired; and the family's boundaries to the outside world have been opened to eliminate their isolation. This is the way new information about problems and how to solve them enters a family system.

If an abusive or incestuous family continues to keep quiet and passively put up with their crazy behavior, nothing will change or, at most, only a first-order change will take place. For example, the wife may divorce her abusing husband only to marry another man who will abuse her. Nothing really changes in such a family script other than the players. Family rules and boundaries remain unchanged.

Family professionals who focus too heavily on coping (adapting) may prevent a family from changing. At least a crisis would mean that the family would have a chance to reorganize. From this perspective, then, *crisis is not always negative; coping is not always positive.* Caution is needed when using either of these terms, so that family professionals do not superimpose their own values (regarding change versus stability) onto the family in stress.

The persistent preference in family research for family coping and invulnerability as an outcome, rather than family conflict and revolt, may be related to the fact that, like most Americans, we value stability and order over chaos and disorder. (The latter is accepted more in Eastern cultural belief systems.) Our Western cultural value of "keeping things under control" and solving all problems may, in fact, lead us to *more* stress, especially when we are faced with stressor events that have no immediate solutions (e.g., chronic illness or pending law suits). Families that pride themselves on being good at solving problems and "taking care of their own" may have a record of coping successes, but they become brittle when they are faced with a stressor event that has no ready solution, a slow terminal illness, for example. In such families a high reliance on control and mastery renders the caregiver and family helpless.

Because they are accustomed to solving anything, such competent families will work and work and work at coping even in the face of a hopeless situation. I see this response in families in which one member has a terminal illness. Some families just work too hard at coping. They would be better off to give up, let go, and face their loss. Once they do this, the grieving process can begin and, ultimately, will lead to something new and different in the family structure.[2] I move in this book, therefore, from a homeostatic model of stress, coping, and adaptation to a theoretical model that incorporates and values the possibilities of change and revolution as much as, if not more than, stability and calm. This dialectic requires *a process view of family stress* (rather than a stable, mechanistic view). I believe things are always in flux in family systems; there is always some tension. If not, you have what therapists call "a dead family" or "a dead marriage." For these reasons, coping, as the term is applied in family literature, may not always be of value to everyone in a stressed family. Use the term with caution.

SOME COMPLEXITIES ABOUT COPING TO ADD TO PREVIOUS CAUTIONS

Although coping increases the ability to withstand stress, we previously cautioned that coping can *increase* vulnerability if adaptations have harmful side effects. Like stress, coping can have both positive and negative consequences for individuals and families. Sometimes, therefore, a radical change in family behavior is preferable to coping and adaptation. For example, a battered wife who leaves her husband may be coping more positively than the beaten wife who somehow learns to tolerate the abuse. On the other hand, the wife of an alcoholic who copes by becoming a workaholic may have chosen a behavior that is not functional. It causes her to feel exhausted. Most of the time this coping strategy increases her vulnerability even beyond the direct effects of her husband's unavailability due to alcoholism.

A behavior, therefore, can be simultaneously a coping mechanism and a stressor event. For example, the family researcher and therapist need to determine whether a mother's employment outside the home is a coping mechanism *or* a stressor event. Certainly, her outside work may *relieve* stress in the family system, economically or psychologically, but on the other hand, it may *increase* stress because of her role overload or her absence. More realistically, both may be happening at the same time. A dialectical rather than categorical view of the event of changing women's roles and, particularly, women's employment, is a more productive and, indeed, less biased approach. Too often the bias toward homeostasis in explaining stress in the families of employed mothers is apparent in both researchers and therapists. Certainly, cultural and socioeconomic contexts need to be considered in such interpretations. What increases stress in the family of one employed mother may not do so in another. Caution is needed here.

The phenomenon of family violence also should be investigated on a more general theoretical level in terms of family stress and coping. As sociologist Richard Gelles (Gelles & Cornell, 1986) has stated, family violence can be a coping mechanism, albeit a dysfunctional one. Violent behavior, in fact, can stem from an inadequate repertoire of behaviors with which to manage stress, which means that the process of functional coping never begins. Family violence and other forms of family dysfunction (e.g., alcoholism, anorexia, bulimia, obesity, shoplifting, suicide, or somatization) can be analyzed more productively from a dialectical perspective by researchers and clinicians, given that these families and the coping behaviors they foster may be simultaneously a way to cope with stress and a stimulus for even more stress.

In the face of the two opposing truths that often operate in families, I have found that the complexity of family systems interaction is best accommodated by the dialectical view. For example, a man may get drunk and hit his wife in order to cope with a frustrating day on the job, or a woman may become an addict (e.g., by the abuse of food, tranquilizers, or work) in order to cope with marital frustrations. In such cases, the coping mechanism selected stimulates the development of even more stress. Family vulnerability increases when such coping behaviors are used so frequently that they become stress producers rather than stress reducers for family members. Work, food, alcohol, shopping, and medication—even sex—can all fall into this category.

THE CHAIN REACTION OF STRESSOR EVENTS

The complexity of a *chain reaction* concept, first described by Scherz (1966), also needs attention as we discuss coping.[3] Families that appear to be coping may not really have resolved the issue and, years later, may manifest the crisis when a similar event triggers past memories. As in atomic fission, the chain of old events can be "set off" again by a new event. The chain reaction phenomenon shows up only when a current loss or separation reactivates an *earlier* family loss that was never fully grieved or resolved. Although many clinicians have observed this phenomenon, there is little empirical evidence to document it because of its complexity and unconscious characteristics. In 1979, Klaus Riegel, a developmental psychologist and dialectician, referred to the "codetermination of events." These are events that occur in one dimension but can precede, trigger, or cause events in another dimension.

As a family therapist, I saw a family who appeared to have coped with their child's being killed; however, they fell into crisis 10 years later when President John F. Kennedy was shot. While they watched the funeral and process of grieving on television, they fell apart and became unable to function. In this chain reaction of events, the event of the loss of a national figure triggered the earlier, more private loss of their own child. Indeed, television reports of losses and grieving may often trigger such chain reactions in individuals and families with unresolved losses.

The phenomena of chain reaction and codetermination must be studied further, because families that appear to be coping may not really have managed their stress. Researchers, for practical reasons, have focused on coping with the stressor events at the moment or a few years past; the complexity goes deeper than that. Many of the data regarding unresolved events are hidden under the family's denial system or in the unconscious of family members.

The implication of this chain reaction phenomenon for family professionals is that we may be zeroing in on an event that is, in fact, not the real stressor. Recently, I saw a young woman who was in crisis. She had just had an abortion so I assumed that this event was the cause of her crisis. When she resisted, I listened more carefully and heard her real pain: She had had to go through the abortion *alone*; she had been abandoned *again*. Her parents did not protect her when she was a child, her boyfriend abandoned her now, and her therapist was out of town. She was alone. As I heard her more clearly, I realized I had been focusing on the wrong event. Fortunately, she persisted.

Too often family professionals think they know what is stressing individuals and families. I thought I knew in the case of the young woman. I was wrong. Often, coping strategies and intervention have to center on the original events rather than on the more obvious triggering event in a chain reaction.

FAMILY COPING RESOURCES

The family's coping resources are its individual and collective *strengths* at the time the stressor event occurs. Examples are economic security, health, intelligence, job skills, proximity of support, spirit of cooperation in the family, relationship skills, and network and social supports. The family's resources, therefore, are the economic, psychological, and physical *assets* upon which members can draw in response to a single stressor event or an accumulation of events.

Having resources, however, does not imply *whether* or *how* a family will use them. For example, a family may use a resource such as money to deal with the event of unemployment in a dysfunctional way (e.g., buy more liquor or a bigger television set) or, more functionally, to train for another job. Thus the availability and amount of family resources remains a static (nonprocess) variable that can rather easily be quantified by researchers and therapists. The qualitative study of *how* and *why* families use their coping resources is, however, another matter and has, to date, not been done. Inasmuch as family cultural values and belief systems as well as gender socialization are foci of qualitative assessments, such research studies are definitely needed.

FAMILY COPING AS OUTCOME: A NEW TERM NEEDED TO AVOID CONFUSION

Based on our discussion in this chapter, coping is more than a resource; it is also an outcome variable. The family either copes or is in crisis. There is, therefore, potential for confusion and circular reasoning.

The family's response to a situation of stress is either crisis *or* managing the degree of stress present. This outcome has the potential at any time to change (see Figure 2.4). When the family recognizes that it has a problem, it brings its coping resources (as in the B factor) into action and the management process is begun. If the family members have few resources, individually and collectively, or if they do not use the coping resources they possess, the family stress management process may *never* begin and crisis (X factor) may result.

This distinction between coping as family resources and coping as the dynamic outcome of a process is critical if we are to avoid circular reasoning. The two are not the same. To avoid confusion, therefore, I recommend the term *managing* instead of *coping* for the outcome term. "The family is managing" is, I believe, a clearer statement than "The family is coping."[4]

As you can see in Figure 2.4, I have changed Hill's original definition of the X factor in the ABC-X model to mean the outcome in *degree of stress* (high to low) or crisis. Unless crisis occurs, the family is managing its level of stress. Managing high stress is an alternative outcome to crisis.

POINTS TO REMEMBER

(1) Coping is the *management* of a stressful event or situation by the family as a unit with no detrimental effects on *any* individual in that family. Family coping is the cognitive, affective, and behavioral process by which individuals and their family system as a whole manage (rather than eradicate) a stressful event or situation.

(2) Stressor events are inevitable in family life; thus the ability to cope is important in ascertaining which families are invulnerable to crisis. There is a major caution, however: Coping does not always mean

health for the family. Sometimes going into crisis is better than adapting over and over again.

(3) Stressor events, although in themselves benign, may stimulate the production of stress levels in the family that must be managed if crisis is to be averted. It is valuable to study highly stressed families and individuals to determine how they manage stress without detrimental effects to either the individual or family. It is also necessary to study those families that failed to cope, fell into crisis, but recovered.

(4) Since coping is a process involving *cognitive, emotional,* and *behavioral* responses of *individuals* as well as the *family* as a collective, assessment of the coping process by family professionals must include responses from *both* the individuals and family as a whole if we are to have valid information on how families manage stress.

(5) In this coping process, the internal context of the family system is salient, especially regarding valuing passivity over mastery and using denial as a family coping mechanism.

(6) Family resources are not the same as coping strategies. Families with many resources may have trouble coping with stress. It is not always true that rich families can cope better with stress than poorer families.

(7) In order to avoid confusion, the term *managed* (versus *crisis*) may be clearer as an outcome variable for the stressed family than *coped* (versus *crisis*). The family's managing stress may be a clearer goal than is coping.

(8) I present a caution about the concept of active coping as being always desirable. This is also a feminist issue, since women have stereotypically been the great adapters in families and cultures. They are the smoothers of troubled waters; they have been expected to fit in and not make waves.

NOTES

1. During the 1970s, much of this research took place at the Center for Prisoner of War Studies (CPWS) at the San Diego Naval Health Research Institute. Directors of the Center were Hamilton McCubbin and Edna Hunter; Richard Rahe was at the Naval Health Institute at this time and Reuben Hill was a consultant to the center. Charles Figley and I, among others, conducted specific research projects at CPWS. For more information, see Boss, 1977, 1980b; Figley, 1978; Hunter, 1983; McCubbin, Dahl, Lester, & Boss, 1975; McCubbin, Dahl, & Hunter, 1976.

2. See Peter Marris (1974) for a detailed discussion on this topic.

3. It is important to note that the more qualitative chain reaction phenomenon is not the same as the quantitative concept of stress pileup as operationalized by Vaughn, Egeland, Sroufe, and Waters (1979) and McCubbin, Boss, Wilson, and Lester (1980). The chain reaction phenomenon is more psychologically based and is more concerned with

impact than with number of events. Stress pileup is primarily the summing up of the events that have happened to the family over a particular period of time.

4. The same issue has haunted theorists working on family problem solving. There needs to be a distinction between "problem solving as an activity" and "solving the problem as an outcome" (David Klein, University of Notre Dame, personal communication, March 1986). Klein has also suggested that the best way to avoid confusion is to use or create separate terms, one for the activity itself and one for the consequences. Therefore, I suggest *coping* as the activity and *management* as the outcome.

FURTHER READING

Antonovsky, A. (1979). *Health, stress and coping.* San Francisco: Jossey-Bass.

Billings, A., & Moos, R. H. (1981). The role of coping responses and social resources in attenuating the stress of life events. *Journal of Behavioral Medicine, 10,* 57-189.

Boss, P. G., McCubbin, H. I., & Lester, G. (1979, March). The corporate executive wife's coping patterns in response to routine husband-father absence. *Family Process, 18,* 79-86.

Cobb, S. (1974). A model for life events and their consequences. In B. S. Dohrenwend & B. P. Dohrenwend (Eds.), *Stressful life events: Their nature and effects.* New York: John Wiley.

Coelho, G., Hamburg, D., & Adams, J. (Eds.). (1974). *Coping and adaptation.* New York: Basic Books.

Cohen, F. (1975). *Psychological preparation, coping and recovery from surgery.* Unpublished doctoral dissertation, University of California, Berkeley.

Hunter, E. J. (1983). Treating the military captive family. In F. Kaslow & R. Ridenour (Eds.), *The military family: Dynamics and treatment.* New York: Guilford Press.

Klein, D., & Hill, R. (1979). Determinants of problem-solving effectiveness. In W. Burr, R. Hill, F. I. Nye, & I. Reiss (Eds.), *Contemporary theories about the family* (Vol. 1). New York: Free Press.

Lazarus, R. S. (1966). *Psychological stress and the coping process.* New York: McGraw-Hill.

Lazarus, R. S. (1976). *Patterns of adjustment* (3rd ed.). New York: McGraw- Hill.

McCubbin, H. (1979, August). Integrating coping behavior in family stress theory. *Journal of Marriage and the Family, 41,* 237-244.

McCubbin, H., Boss, P., Wilson, L., & Lester, G. (1980). Developing family invulnerability to stress: Coping patterns and strategies wives employ. In J. Trost (Ed.), *The family and change.* Sweden: International Library.

McCubbin, H., Dahl, B., Lester, G., Benson, D., & Robertson, M. (1976). Coping repertoires of families adapting to prolonged war-induced separations. *Journal of Marriage and the Family, 38*(3), 471-478.

Menaghan, E. G. (1983). Individual coping efforts and family studies: Conceptual and methodological issues. In H. I. McCubbin, M. B. Sussman, & J. M. Patterson (Eds.), *Social stress and the family.* New York: Haworth Press.

Monat, A., & Lazarus, R. S. (Eds.). (1977). *Stress and coping.* New York: Columbia University Press.

Vaillant, G. E. (1977). *Adaptation to life.* Boston: Little, Brown.

Ventura, J., & Boss, P. G. (1983, November). The Family Coping Inventory applied to parents with new babies. *Journal of Marriage and the Family, 45,* 867-875.

Wortman, C. (1983). Coping with victimization: Conclusions and implications for future research. *Journal of Social Issues, 39,* 195-221.

CHAPTER

4

Boundary Ambiguity:
A Barrier to Family Stress Management

THE FAMILY'S INTERNAL CONTEXT

Families do not live in a vacuum; they function within a larger environment. In order for us to understand and make predictions about families in stress, we must first consider their contexts.

Chapters 4, 5, and 6 are devoted to a close examination of the *internal* context of families in stress (see Figure 2.3). Chapter 7 focuses on the *external* context. The greater space given to the internal context does not mean that it is more important than the external; both are critical in determining which families manage stress and which experience crisis. The family's internal context is, however, malleable and therefore of direct interest to those interested in easing family problems. Change in the internal context lies under the control of the individual family and its members, whereas the family's external context is composed of things the family cannot control—global politics, macroeconomics, genetics, maturation, and place in history.

Some families, of course, try to change their external context; the most heroic examples are the MIA families who, in 1976, picketed the Paris Peace Talks to bring to national and international attention the plight of the POW and MIA families. They made some progress with this effort, but 12 years later, despite their heroic efforts, they are still overpowered by the forces of international politics, which unfortunately show little concern for the stress of individual families.

Change in the family's internal context, however, is possible. The family has more control here.[1] The internal context of the family is made up of three micro dimensions that are classified as structural, psychological, and philosophical. The *structural dimension* refers to the family system boundaries, as defined by the family's perceptions regarding who is in and who is outside those boundaries. Boundary ambiguity is, I believe, a new and major structural variable in the family's internal context. It is the focus of this chapter.

The *psychological dimension* of the family's internal context is illustrated by denial, a defense mechanism that is used frequently by stressed families. An in-depth discussion of family denial is presented in Chapter 5.

The *philosophical dimension* of the family's internal context is examined in Chapter 6. It comprises the family's values and belief systems. All three dimensions of the family's internal context are influenced by the external context. I begin with the structural dimension.

FAMILY BOUNDARY AMBIGUITY

Sometimes a family's perception of a situation is such that the family is prevented from managing stress. One such barrier to the resolution of stress management in families is what I have labeled "boundary ambiguity." In simple terms, it means *not knowing who is in and who is out of the family*. For the most part, boundary ambiguity is negative in its consequences but, indeed, over the short term and in moderate amounts, it is a phenomenon that simply may be a part of everyday life as family members come and go. We need to be able to tolerate short-term ambiguity in family life. My discussion here, however, focuses on families in which the ambiguity is long-term and severe. (See Figure 4.1.)

Family Boundary Maintenance[2]

To define boundary ambiguity I must first define its opposite, family boundary maintenance. In the general systems theory of Walter Buckley (1967), "boundary maintenance" means that the perimeters of a system are secure and well defined. A living organism cannot survive if it does not have a clearly defined boundary. A family is a living organism; it is a living system.

Focusing just on *family* systems, sociologist Joan Aldous in her discussion of boundary maintenance pointed to the paradoxical nature of the concept of family boundary. On the one hand, families tend to establish distinct boundaries through daily interactions, rituals, and terminology. On the other hand, families are often called upon or forced to open their boundaries selectively in order to transact business with economic and social institutions (Aldous, 1978). For example, family members have to go to work or go to school. Reuben Hill pointed out that boundary maintenance problems in families are most likely to occur at developmental transition periods, especially "when the family is launching its young adult members into jobs and marriage [given] the uncertainties about the precise obligations of their attenuated membership in the parental family" (Hill, 1971).

If family boundaries cannot be maintained, they are ambiguous. What precisely does this mean for families?

Two Types of High Family Boundary Ambiguity

When family members are uncertain in their perceptions of *who is in or out of the family system*, the boundaries of the family system are unclear or ambiguous. There are two kinds of high boundary ambiguity; both have been associated with family dysfunction. The first type of high boundary ambiguity (see Figure 4.1) is illustrated by *physical absence with psychological presence*. That is, a family member is physically absent but perceived as psychologically present. There is an emotional preoccupation with the absent family member. The preoccupation persists because facts surrounding that person's whereabouts are unclear. Grieving and restructuring are not possible; so the family is held in limbo. Families of missing children, political hostages, and men still missing in action fit into this category of high boundary ambiguity. Also, some divorced families may fit into this category when one spouse will not recognize the divorce or when a child is preoccupied with the absent parent.

The second type of high boundary ambiguity is *physical presence with psychological absence* (see Figure 4.1). The family is physically intact but one member is emotionally unavailable to the family system. Examples are families having a member in a coma or chronically ill with drug or alcohol addition, Alzheimer's disease, or other forms of dementia, or simply having a family member preoccupied with work demands. The main point in this type of high boundary ambiguity is that the family member is physically present but his or her mind is somewhere else. (See Figure 4.2.)

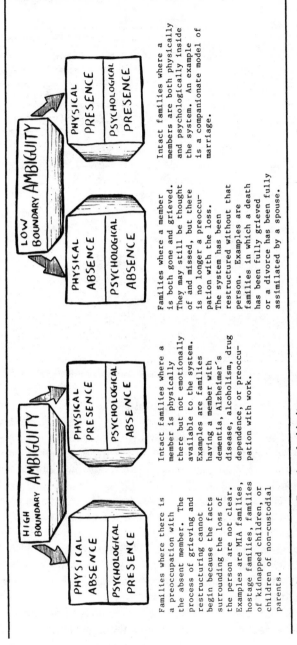

HIGH BOUNDARY AMBIGUITY

PHYSICAL ABSENCE
PSYCHOLOGICAL PRESENCE

PHYSICAL PRESENCE
PSYCHOLOGICAL ABSENCE

Families where there is a preoccupation with the absent member. The process of grieving and restructuring cannot begin because the facts surrounding the loss of the person are not clear. Examples are MIA families, hostage families, families of kidnapped children, or children of non-custodial parents.

Intact families where a member is physically there but not emotionally available to the system. Examples are families having a member with dementia, Alzheimer's disease, alcoholism, drug dependence, or preoccupation with work.

LOW BOUNDARY AMBIGUITY

PHYSICAL ABSENCE
PSYCHOLOGICAL ABSENCE

PHYSICAL PRESENCE
PSYCHOLOGICAL PRESENCE

Families where a member is both gone and grieved. They may still be thought of and missed, but there is no longer a preoccupation with the loss. The system has been restructured without that person. Examples are families in which a death has been fully grieved or a divorce has been fully assimilated by a spouse.

Intact families where a members are both physically and psychologically inside the system. An example is a companionate model of marriage.

Figure 4.1: High and Low Boundary Ambiguity

Figure 4.2

Two Types of Low Boundary Ambiguity

I predict no dysfunction when there is low boundary ambiguity in families (see Figure 4.1). Family members are clear in their perception of who is in or out of the family system, and the boundaries of the system are clear to all family members. The first type of low boundary ambiguity is *physical absence with psychological absence*. There is congruence between being physically and emotionally absent. Although they are still thought of and missed, there is no longer a preoccupation with the missing person. The family has restructured without them. Examples are families in which a death has been clearly recognized and fully grieved or in which a divorce has been fully recognized and assimilated by a spouse.

The second type of low boundary ambiguity is *physical presence with psychological presence*. Being together in body and mind, physically and emotionally, creates a congruence in the family's boundary so that ambiguity is low or nonexistent. Examples would be a companionate model or marriage or a family that is truly an emotional haven for its members.

How Boundary Ambiguity Fits into the Family Stress Model

Relating family boundary ambiguity to the family stress model and conceptual map (Figure 4.3), note that boundary ambiguity can manifest itself under either the stressor event (A factor) or the perception of the event (C factor). That is, family boundary ambiguity can result from two different situations: (a) one in which the facts surrounding the *event* are unclear (e.g., MIA, hostage taking, kidnapping, desertion, Alzheimer's disease, and some divorce situations) or (b) one in which the facts surrounding the event are clear but, for some reason, *the family ignores or denies them* (alcoholism, terminal illness, and so on). In the latter case, the family's perception of the event is different from that of an objective outside observer. The family perceives an ill member as well (alcoholism); they perceive a missing family member as present (MIA); or they perceive a family member as absent while physically present (Alzheimer's disease).

What is of critical importance to researchers, educators, and therapists who want to use the concept of boundary ambiguity is that its effect on family stress stems primarily from *the family's perception of the event* (C factor). That is, it doesn't matter whether the ambiguity results from unavailable facts surrounding the event or from the family's distortion of those facts; it is *the family's perception of the event or situation (the meaning they give it) that is the critical variable in determining the existence and degree of boundary ambiguity.* Thus therapists and researchers must be careful not to be misled by what they see as the presence or absence of facts about an event of loss because the family gives that event its own meaning and reality. The family's perception ultimately determines the degree of boundary ambiguity, which is indicated by the congruence between their *psychological perception* of who is in and who is out with the *physical reality* of who is in and who is out of that system.

For both clinicians and researchers, as well as all of us personally, it is possible to bring a family's perceptions to the surface by simply asking, individually and collectively: Who is in the family? Who is out? Who performs what roles? Who carries out what tasks? Who is included in the family's rituals (weddings, graduations, funerals, holidays, religious events, and so on)? What we find out may not always be what we expected (for more details on measurement, see Boss, Pearce-McCall, & Greenberg, 1988).

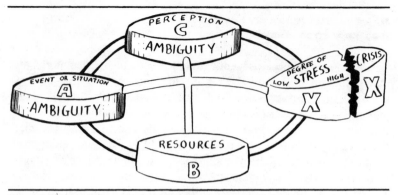

Figure 4.3:   Boundary: Where It Fits into the Family Stress Model

NORMATIVE BOUNDARY AMBIGUITY
IN FAMILIES ACROSS THE LIFE CYCLE

Although boundary ambiguity research began primarily with military families and disaster victims, I also have systematically studied families in more normative situations (Boss et al., 1987). The events of loss and separation that are so common to military families occur, although in different degrees, in normal everyday family life as well. Entries and exits of family members across the family life span are inevitable; thus births, adolescents leaving home for college or work, marriages, retirements, and deaths continuously affect the family system's process of boundary maintenance.

Learning to clarify family boundaries after a loss or acquisition, is therefore, one of the most critical developmental tasks required of families over the life cycle. The task of being able to let go and take in, to adapt to the systemic change that this process of transition demands, is a major coping strategy for *all* families and *all* individuals over the life cycle. Human beings change as they mature; this in itself is a normative stressor to every family system.

If I were to summarize theoretically one task that is universally essential for all family functioning over the life cycle regardless of culture or class, it would be the task of clarifying family boundaries. Although this continual process of boundary maintenance is never perfectly achieved, the family's participation in the process of achieving clarification and maintenance is critical.

The decade of the 1970s saw renewed interest in normative developmental life events that can trigger family stress. Again, researchers in the disciplines of sociology, developmental psychology, and social work participated in the work. Pearlin and Radebaugh (1976) identified major role changes during the life cycle when individuals move through normatively expected entrances into and exits from social roles. They developed "strain scores" to measure the stress of these entrances and exits. Role changes and task realignments during the transition periods in the family life cycle were also the focus of my research (Boss, 1980b, 1983b), and the research of Golan (1978), Hill (1973), Hill and Joy (1979), and Mederer and Hill (1983). The acquisition of roles was found to be more stressful than the loss of roles (George, 1980; Neugarten & Hagestad, 1977); and strain scores related to normative stress were found to be lower than the scores for non-normative events (Pearlin & Lieberman, 1979).

All these normal family events and situations center on the occurrence or perception of *loss*. Sometimes it is the clear-cut loss of a family member by death but, at other times, as in developmental events, it is how the loss of a family member or how the loss of his or her familiar role is perceived. Boundary ambiguity, therefore, results from normal developmental changes across the family life cycle as well as from disasters and the actual physical loss of members.

When an adolescent leaves home, the family *loses* a dependent child but *gains* an independent young adult; when an elderly parent grows frail, the family members *lose* a person they looked up to and leaned on and they *gain* a serious and tender responsibility. When babies grow up and go to school for the first time, the parents *lose* someone exclusively dependent upon them, but *gain* an increasingly independent and self-sufficient offspring.

Whether these changes result in relief or sadness, they represent the loss of something irretrievable. Families cannot go back to the way things were. Human development brings inevitable change; hence family boundaries also change. The perception of who is in and who is out must match those changes if family boundaries are to be maintained.

Giving up and letting go are events that happen to all families across the life span. Families may be fortunate enough to have no disastrous losses; yet they surely will have normative losses. Whether these losses produce crisis or are managed may be determined by the degree and duration of ambiguity in the family boundary after the event occurs. It is for this reason that being able to resolve boundary ambiguity is important in determining whether the family will reorganize and maintain its boundaries as a viable system, whether it will become a system with highly ambiguous boundaries and increased dysfunction. Indeed, this premise may help to explain why some families can manage high stress whereas other families crumble with the least amount. *The ability to clarify and maintain boundaries after loss may be more relevant to predicting whether a family will manage stress or go into crisis than continued focus on the stressor event itself.*

When the Question of
Boundary Ambiguity Becomes Critical

The issue of boundary ambiguity becomes most salient in families at times of transition or change. Specifically, boundary ambiguity comes to the fore when a family member enters or exits the family system. Because of my research on loss, I focus primarily on the exiting of family members.

When a family member who has been in the system leaves, the system must reorganize in order to make up for the void. This happens when a family member leaves for normative reasons (an adolescent going off to college or an aged grandparent dies), or it can occur unexpectedly, for example, when a family member is killed in an accident or when a member runs away from home.

Despite the major differences in these examples, the family boundary is disturbed in all cases by the loss of the member. When the family boundary is in disequilibrium, family stress is higher. Simply put, the family boundary is disturbed and no longer maintained. A reorganization or restructuring is needed before the level of family stress will subside. The family will experience boundary ambiguity until a new equilibrium is reached in one of two ways: physically (the person returns or someone else is taken in by the family as a replacement) or perceptually (the family decides to reconcile themselves to the loss by shifting perceptions and assigning the vacated roles in the system to other members who are physically there). One could say that because family transitions across the life cycle are inevitable and, indeed, desirable, boundary ambiguity is as much functional as dysfunctional. Clinicians know this is true. Ambiguity in family life is inevitable; we cannot always control and know precisely what is happening to us. For both individuals and families as a whole, then, tolerance for some ambiguity is a sign of maturity and good mental health.

There is a limit in degree and time to how much ambiguity a person or family can tolerate, however. To be sure, a healthy family and mature parents should be able to endure the ambiguity during the years an adolescent is gaining independence and being launched. But it is another matter to say that individuals and families ought to be able to tolerate the decades of ambiguity in their family's boundary that is caused when a family member is missing in action, kidnapped, taken hostage, or gone and no one has any knowledge of the individual's condition or whereabouts. Long-term boundary ambiguity is virtually intolerable for even the strongest of families. Certainly the most challenged in our lifetime have been the MIA families.

Just as the physical loss of a family member causes ambiguity in the family boundary, so too does a member's psychological absence. People can be missing psychologically as well as physically. For example, children of alcoholics report experiencing confusion and high stress because a parent is there in body but not there in mind. The alcoholic is physically present in the home but, because of the disease, he or she is psychologically absent. Long-term boundary ambiguity is very difficult for children to manage, and they may carry the effects of it into adulthood. Were the psychological absence of a shorter duration— perhaps a day or a week, as when we are home but preoccupied with writing a paper, reading a book, or getting ready for a contest—this ambiguity could be tolerated.

People can be missing psychologically as well as physically, but it is when the boundary ambiguity is long-term that families find absences difficult to manage. In either case, families may have to decide what the reality is for them if they cannot get facts about the missing family members. To be sure, this represents a "family gamble."

The Family Gamble

Sometimes when a family cannot get the facts about the whereabouts of a family member or the status of someone who is chronically ill, they take it upon themselves to gamble (make a decision choice) on whether that person *is in or out of the family system.* When a family member is consistently "missing," psychologically or physically, the rest of the family may decide to "close the individual out" and to proceed with family life as if he or she were not there. While someone is missing (psychologically or physically), the family is in limbo. They are unable to grieve their loss because they don't know if that person is "in or out of the family." After they have been in limbo for a time and unsuccessful in their attempts to bring back the missing person, the family may decide to conclude that the missing person is indeed gone and no longer available to them. They begin to grieve their loss. This perception can be agreed upon in the absence of definite facts. I have observed similar structural decisions in families of the missing-in-action, Alzheimer's disease, and other chronic illnesses, such as alcoholism.

Sometimes a family makes a mistake in their gamble to find reality. The missing person returns after years of absence; so the family has to reopen its boundaries to let him or her back in. A missing person is found. An addicted person goes into treatment and wants to rejoin the family. Such changes, however, although positive, also can cause increased stress in families, especially in those who had closed out the missing person. Getting family members back as well as losing them can produce stress for families. Both loss and acquisition disturb the equilibrium and require a reorganization not only of boundaries but of all systems interaction as well.

In some families, such as MIA families, the change is not so clear-cut. Their missing member does not return and they are not sure whether he or she is dead. They only hear reports of sightings in the jungle or of bodies that may be returned to them. In such families, the phenomenon of boundary ambiguity remains high as long as the family's agreed-upon perception is threatened by new information. When there are reports of missing persons being seen alive, of remains being found, or of hostages being sighted, ambiguity grows as each report increases the prospect of another boundary change. Whether positive or negative, any prospect of change disturbs family boundary maintenance. Having been clarified by a family gamble, the boundary is *once again* ambiguous. *Once again*, the family is unsure if the lost person is in or out of the system. *Once again*, the gamble has been made. It causes extremely high stress and taxes even the strongest of families.

Two Situations in Which There Is High Potential for Boundary Ambiguity

Events differ between MIA and divorced families, but they have in common the potential for boundary ambiguity. Although one event grows out of disaster and the other is normative, in both cases the status of the absent parent within the family boundary is unclear. I identified theoretical parallels in an earlier paper (Boss, 1983a) that may help to explain the disturbance on the family system brought about by these situations.

(1) Both events represent a loss of membership, either psychological, physical, or both, and, therefore, a change in the family system boundary.

(2) Both events represent an unclear loss (i.e., it is not absolutely clear to family members whether the absent parent is in or out of the family system or in or out of what roles).

(3) No social rituals clarify either event of loss (missing-in-action or divorce) as they do when a spouse dies (families, therefore, must find their own way to manage the loss without support and guidance from social rituals).

(4) Both events involve different types of role assignments, that is, instrumental (task oriented) or expressive (socioemotional), thus close-out and clarification of family boundary may not be total. The psychological or emotional close-out of the missing person may precede the close-out of his or her instrumental role, especially that of providing economic support for the children. In divorced families, the instrumental role of providing money often continues from the absent parent, just as it did in some MIA families, when wives decided to accept the missing husband's paycheck as long as children were young and still at home. Acceptance of economic support was not found to be dysfunctional as long as individual family members were clear about the roles in which the absent parent remained active and those that were closed out (see Boss, 1977).

(5) Both events involve the loss of one family leader. Thus a major reorganization to a single-parent system is needed for boundary maintenance in divorced as well as MIA families. This means the remaining or custodial parent must act in *both* instrumental and expressive leadership roles. If gender socialization did not provide the preparation for this dual leadership role in the family, he or she will now have to learn this. Women may need to become more instrumental and men more expressive if they are to lead a family alone.

Some of the research upon which the theoretical concept of boundary ambiguity is based is reviewed in Chapter 5.

POINTS TO REMEMBER

(1) Families are systems. Systems must maintain their boundaries if they are to survive and not collapse under pressure.

(2) Family boundaries cannot be maintained by outsiders; they must be maintained from the inside, by the family itself. Clear and healthy family boundaries facilitate the management of stressful family life events and the family is better able to manage inevitable, normative loss and change. Clear boundaries enable a family to resolve changes as its members develop over time. It can also better manage unexpected events or situations.

(3) In order for a family system to maintain its boundaries, the family members must know *who is in and who is outside the family*. This is

determined by asking each family member for an individual and then a collective perception of who is in the family. It is also determined by asking who is present at times of family celebrations and rituals.

(4) The significant barrier to family stress management then is not so much the events of loss (or acquisition), but the ambiguity caused when *we do not know if the person is in or out of the family system.*

(5) Some degree of ambiguity is normal in the family, but long-term ambiguity is a severe stressor and will make vulnerable even the strongest of families.

(6) Although the idea of boundary ambiguity as dysfunctional grew out of the MIA family research, it appears to have relevance for more normative family events of loss such as divorce and adolescents' leaving home.

(7) When an event of loss cannot be changed, change is still possible in the family's *perception* of that event.

NOTES

1. I emphasize the micro (internal context) because it allows the most change for families; however, the macro view is also critical and should not be underestimated. An excellent book that takes the macro point of view is *Family Politics* by Lettie Cottin Pogrebin (1983); it was written for educators, politicians, policymakers, and economists.

2. The concept of boundary ambiguity captures only one aspect of boundaries that is relevant to family stress theory. There are others: Vern Bengtson's "developmental stake" notion, for example, highlights the differences between parents and adolescent over an adolescent's role and status in the family. Both generations may be absolutely certain about their positions; they just see things differently. David Klein pointed out that such opposing views are "boundary conflict." We also have the variables of ambivalence and boundary permeability. None of these three variables is what I mean by "boundary ambiguity," however. Although they are valid variables in family stress theory, they are not what I am describing here. Boundary ambiguity is a newly conceived variable in family stress theory. For a discussion of its antecedents in the literature of sociology, social psychology, and family therapy, see Boss and Greenberg (1984).

FURTHER READING

Ahrons, C. R., & Rogers, R. H. (1987). *Divorced families.* New York: McGraw-Hill.

Boss, P. G. (1975b). Psychological father presence in the missing-in-action (MIA) family: Its effects on family functioning. *Proceedings: Third Annual Joint Medical Meeting Concerning POW/MIA Matters* (pp. 61-65). Center for Prisoner of War Studies, Naval Health Research Center, San Diego, November.

Boss, P. G. (1977, February). A clarification of the concept of psychological father presence in families experiencing ambiguity of boundary. *Journal of Marriage and the Family, 39,* 141-151.

25

Boss, P. G. (1980a). Normative family stress: Family boundary changes across the lifespan. *Family Relations, 29*, 445-450.

Boss, P. G. (1980b). The relationship of psychological father presence, wife's personal qualities, and wife/family dysfunction in families of missing fathers. *Journal of Marriage and the Family, 42*(3), 541-549.

Boss, P. G. (1980c). Précis prepared for the emergency meeting of the Task Force on Families of Catastrophe, February 4-5, 1980. In C. R. Figley (Ed.), *Mobilization: Part I. The Iranian crisis. Final report of the Task Force on Families of Catastrophe.* West Lafayette, IN: Family Research Institute, Purdue University.

Boss, P. G. (1983a). Family separation and boundary ambiguity. In O. Hultaker & J. Trost (Eds.), Family and disaster [Special issue]. *International Journal of Mass Emergencies and Disasters, 1*(1), 63-72.

Boss, P. G. (1983b). The marital relationship: Boundaries and ambiguities. In C. Figley & H. I. McCubbin (Eds.), *Stress and the family* (Vol. 2). New York: Brunner/Mazel.

Boss, P. G., & Greenberg, J. (1984). Family boundary ambiguity: A new variable in family stress theory. *Family Process, 23*, 535-546.

Boss, P., Caron, W., & Horbal, J. (1988). Alzheimer's disease and ambiguous loss. In C. Chilman, F. Cox, & E. Nunnally (Eds.), *Families in trouble.* Newbury Park, CA: Sage.

Boss, P., Pearce-McCall, D., & Greenberg, J. (1988). *The measurement of boundary ambiguity in families: Research instrument* (Agricultural Extension Service publication). St. Paul: Family Social Science Department, University of Minnesota.

CHAPTER
5

Denial:
Another Barrier to Family Stress Management

THE CONCEPT OF DENIAL has received less attention from researchers than from clinicians who, since the time of Sigmund Freud, have recognized its existence and power in families. Denial is *the refusal to believe what one sees*. It is the refusal to believe or accept a physical reality. Others can see what is happening but not persons or families who deny the happenings. It is commonly accepted that denial is a defense mechanism in which external reality is rejected. It should be noted that a person's culture and value orientation influence *what* is unacceptable to see and thus *what* events are denied. A family's context, therefore, determines whether denial is used in response to stressful events or situations.

The function of denial is debatable. It is dysfunctional when it prevents cognitive preparation for an event of separation and thereby blocks family reorganization and holds the family system in an unresolved state. In essence, denial allows the individual or family to defend the status quo; everything is the same as it always was; nothing has changed. The following anecdotes illustrate dysfunctional uses of denial:

Dad lost his job the other day. I know because it was in the paper that the factory shut down. He acts as if nothing has changed, getting up in the morning and pretending to go off to work as usual. I wonder where he goes all day. When he comes home for supper, we can tell he's depressed. Why doesn't he just talk about losing his job? It would be easier on us than this pretending.

Dad and Mom got divorced over a year ago, but it's like she still expects him to come back. She doesn't make any friends of her own. Worse yet,

"SORRY MY FATHER ISN'T HERE RIGHT NOW..."

Figure 5.1

she won't make any decision without trying to call him to see what he says, and then they just get into a fight again. So she asks me what to do. What can I say? I'm just a kid! She's got to admit he's gone and learn to make her own decisions. I can't stand it anymore. I'm thinking about getting out of here.

Mom and Dad are fighting all the time, especially after they have a few drinks. It gets really violent and I get really scared that they'll hurt each other. After it's all over, they act like nothing happened, smiling at each other and holding hands. When I ask them what's going on, they act like I've asked a stupid question. "Why, nothing's wrong. Why would you think that?" It makes me feel like I'm going crazy.

Denial can also be functional for the family, however, especially in the early stages of a stressful event. For example, it may take a few hours or days, or even a month or two to get used to the idea that a job has been lost, that a mate has left, or that someone who was loved has died. If we were to be diagnosed as having a terminal illness, our first reaction probably would be to deny that fact.

Almost two decades ago, Elisabeth Kübler-Ross (1969), a noted Swiss psychiatrist, said that denial is the first stage of the grieving process. She considered denial, at least for a time, a healthy way of dealing with an uncomfortable and painful situation because it served as a buffer after unexpected shocking news. A period of denial "allows people to collect themselves and, with time, mobilize other, less radical defenses" (p. 39).

A family faced with the terminal illness of a member undergoes similar stages of adjustment. At first the family may deny the fact of terminal illness in the family or "shop around" from doctor to doctor in the vain hope of hearing that the diagnosis was wrong. According to Kübler-Ross,

> They may seek help and reassurance that it is all not true from fortune-tellers and faith healers. They may arrange for expensive trips to famous clinics and physicians and only gradually face up to the reality that may change their life so drastically. (p. 168)

Depending upon the patient's perception and attitude and the family's ability to communicate, the family may suddenly shift its perception to an acceptance of reality and a recognition of the impending loss. The family secret, painful as it is, is revealed and recognized, explicitly. Family members talk and cry together and perform the necessary tasks to prepare for the loss (Kübler-Ross, 1969). Although breaking their denial system also causes pain, the family is now recognizing reality and preparing for the future.

The big question about denial in families is this: Does denial prevent cognition and family stress management, or is it a cognitive decision at some level to manage by ignoring reality? If denial of a loss prevents the cognitive preparation for grieving and subsequent reorganization, then the outcome of the denial is dysfunctional. If denial is in itself a purposeful decision to "freeze" the process of grieving, for example, in the case of ambiguous loss when the Iranian hostages were being held, then denial may have a positive influence on outcome, at least in the short term. For example, not knowing if their loved ones would return safely, the families of Iranian hostages gambled on a safe return and kept their family members psychologically present (Boss, 1980c). They remembered their birthdays, storing gift packages for when they returned; talked to them on tapes and in letters even if they could not be delivered; and denied a negative outcome, hoping for their safe return. The Americans taken hostage did in fact return; so the denial of loss and maintenance of their places in the family systems were functional. The families in this case won the gamble.

When there is no way to change a stressor event or when a situation of loss is certain, a family's use of denial and the maintenance of hope are related. Individually or as a group, they deny that the event is hopeless in order to keep open the possibility that loss will not occur. Families often go to great lengths to keep this status quo, to avoid painful change. Only when they finally accept the fact of *hopelessness* can they stop using denial. They stop gambling and face the reality of their loss.

Denial also can be functional in lowering physiological stress. One's heart rate or blood pressure can be calmed if a stressor event is denied (Wolff, Friedman, Hofer, & Mason, 1964). Sometimes, however, lowered physiological stress is accompanied by serious psychological consequences. If family members convince each other that "there is really nothing wrong with Dad," then their stress level will go down, but, if their father knows his illness is terminal, his stress level will rise when no one in the family allows him to talk about it.

From the literature, it is clear that a response that is optimal in one situation at one time may be damaging in some other situation or at a different time. For example, denial may be effective in the physiological domain (i.e., lowering secretions of stress-related hormones) for parents of a terminally ill child prior to the child's death (Wolff et al., 1964), but denial may prove ineffective after the child dies (i.e., stress-related hormones then increase dramatically because the reality of the child's death broke their denial [Hofer, Wolff, Friedman, & Mason, 1972]). Clearly, whether denial is considered a beneficial response is highly dependent upon the situational timing, according to stress researchers Monat and Lazarus (1977).

Traditionally, denial, when it is used to cover up a stressor event, is a palliative mode of coping and is maladaptive (Lazarus, 1977). Family therapists also view such family cover-ups as dysfunctional and work to break the denial systems. If Mom is denying a lump in her breast, she must see a doctor; if Dad has had too many drinks at a party and still insists on driving home, he must be challenged. Active coping and managing means going to a doctor when you have to or letting a friend drive you home when you are not capable of driving safely.

Nevertheless, denial is a useful defense in many situations, at least initially, in that it prevents a person or a family from being overwhelmed by a situation in which immediate direct action is limited or of little use (Hamburg & Adams, 1967). Finding out that a family member has a terminal illness may be too much to accept right away. The family may need a few hours or days to accept that information. When they can do nothing to change the event or threat, denying that it is there may be momentarily helpful while gaining strength and the sense of what to do and how to proceed. A family can go into "shock" just as the body does after trauma; the family needs time to process and face the stressor event. Denial buys them a little time. The big question is, how much?

Though sparse, the literature that answers this question appears to be consistent: Denial is more likely to be a useful mechanism for stress management in the *short term* and harmful in the *long term* (Cohen, 1975; Hamburg & Adams, 1967). As a family therapist, I would agree. Cohen added that short-term denial is useful in situations (a) when a person would be overwhelmed by an unpleasant reality; (b) when the likelihood of the threat actually occurring is small; (c) when an individual can do nothing to prepare for the potential threatening event; and (d) when a hopeful attitude prevents feelings of giving up (1975).

Monat and Lazarus (1977) also emphasized the importance of *time* and *situation* in ascertaining the positive or negative effects of denial as a mechanism for managing stress. They wrote that a palliative (cover-up) mode of coping (e.g., denial) may be damaging when it prevents essential direct actions, but it may be extremely useful in helping a person to maintain a sense of well-being, integration, or hope under conditions otherwise likely to encourage psychological disintegration (p. 10). The observation is also true for families, but only for a short time. If a cover-up mode of coping, such as denial, is used too long, the family boundary cannot be maintained and the family will become dysfunctional.

Here are some examples. We frequently see denial in family systems in which a member is suffering from a slow but fatal disease. The illness is both grave and ambiguous in outcome. The patient will die but no one knows when. Therefore, the families frequently manage by denying either the illness or the presence of the family member who is ill. They act as if he or she already is dead and gone. In such a terminal chronic illness, the threat of loss remains "a potent aspect of the family's experience for an indefinite period of time" and "little, if any, of this negative feeling can be expressed openly because the patient is gravely ill and cannot be blamed for the situation" (Gonzalez & Reiss, 1981, p. 6). The family is then left little choice but to deny the reality of the situation. By denying the problem, they appear to "buy time."

However, when a family member's status is chronically ambiguous (one does not know if the individual is in or out of the family system), reorganization of the family system is impossible. Change cannot take place because the status of family membership and boundaries lacks clarity. In order to maintain morale and gain time until more evidence accumulates, the family may need to deny reality.

The early extrusion of a physically present family member from the family system, as reported by Gonzalez and Reiss (1981), demonstrates the qualitative impact of ambiguous loss on family system boundaries. Denying the existence of the disease keeps the chronically ill member inside the family system, whereas acknowledging the inevitable result of the illness may precipitate "a closing out" (Boss, 1977), "a closing of ranks" (Hill, 1949), or "a premature extrusion" (Gonzalez & Reiss, 1981) of that member from the family system. I find the same phenomenon of denial at work in families of members with Alzheimer's disease. I predict it will also be found in families of AIDS patients.

The studies of ambiguity in stressful situations have focused primarily on populations where the stressor event itself contains the ambiguity. That is, the family cannot get clear facts about the event, as in missing-in-action (MIA), end-stage-renal-disease (ESRD), or Alzheimer's disease; thus they do not know if the affected family member is in or out of the family. Inasmuch as boundary ambiguity in such instances is caused and maintained by the event itself, *denial may be the only coping mechanism available to the family*. In the absence of clear facts and the inability to control the situation, a family simply may manage by denying reality and reconstructing what is happening, based on their wishful thinking (e.g., "Mother really isn't sick; everything is as it always was; there is nothing hurtful here; no one is going to die" or "that person isn't really a member of our family anyhow").

In other situations, however, the facts regarding family membership are clear, but some family members (or all) still continue to deny or ignore facts. In such cases, the ambiguity is internally supported because, for example, a parent *perceptually* maintains a fictional boundary despite a death certificate. Perhaps because such families are more likely to become dysfunctional, we see examples of them frequently in family therapy. Denial, therefore, is relevant in both situations of family boundary ambiguity: that caused by the event itself and that caused by perception only. But, like the variable of boundary ambiguity, the existence or nonexistence of denial flows ultimately from the C factor, the family's perception of the event. Regardless of the unavailability of facts about an event or situation, the family's perception of it is what must be assessed if we are to understand what an event of loss *means* to a family and how they can subsequently manage it.

HOW SOME FAMILIES BREAK THROUGH DENIAL

When families finally admit there is a problem, they can begin to talk about it, burst the bubble, and dare to say the unspeakable. Most often, this process starts with one person:

Kids, I'm out of work. Your mom and I are trying to figure out a way to make ends meet during these hard times. There is barely enough money for the essentials. Can you help us by not asking for extras and by even helping to earn some money in whatever way you can, or in doing some of the jobs at home so that Mom can go to work? She can get a job right now easier than I can, so we are going to have to reorganize some jobs around here. If we stick together and work as a team, we can survive. That means I have to do the housework and Mom has to get a job. It means you'll also have to help. Let's all of us sit down and talk about what to do.

Dad, I love you, but I don't like the way you act when you're drunk. I would like you to stop because I care about you. If you don't stop, I won't hang around since it hurts me too much to see you that way.

Mom, as your kid, I have to tell you that I can't stand watching you and Dad fight any more. If you don't call the cops the next time Dad hits you, I will.

Grandpa, I know how sick you are. I just want you to know that I love you and that I will miss you when you die. Is there anything I can do for you now?

Another way families break through the barrier of denial is to gather all the facts possible about the event: What are the chances for recovery or reversal of the loss? Is there hope? What are the alternatives? If nothing can be done about the situation and if there is absolutely no hope for reversal, they can talk about grieving and eventually reorganizing: Who can cover the jobs that need to be done in the family? What needs to be done to make the family work right now? Are there community resources that could help? Where can they get the information and help they need?

If most family members refuse to face facts and still deny the loss, even one member can confront the situation and gather more facts. If the family still denies reality, that member may need to take care of him- or herself, making major changes, such as learning new skills or moving to a new place. Usually, it is one family member who breaks through the denial pattern first and, if allowed to talk freely, will break the family's "unspoken secret" open for everyone. Painful as it is, this action is the beginning of family reorganization and health. Lower stress and better health then become possible for them despite their loss. The family talks together, perhaps cries together, and then reorganizes their family boundary, taking into account their loss. The stress level in families that do not break through this denial system only goes higher.

A final way families break through the denial system is to recognize the hopelessness of the situation and give up. Once the family realizes the event cannot be changed, they can accept it. As one wife on the Minnesota Iron Range said, "It does no good to continue to beat my head against a brick wall. My husband can't get his job back so we have to give up on mining and find another solution." After investigating other options, they talked to others to find out *new* ways to make a living and relocated as Dad trained for a new job in the health care industry. Rather than denying that the mining job had been lost, they faced a fact that could not be changed (taconite is no longer in demand) and, instead, changed the way they looked at the situation. This is how another father, now out of work, was finally able to talk about his family's management of stress:

> Our family income is lower, but it doesn't mean I'm less of a person just because I lost my job. If I can't earn all the money we need, then other family members will have to help—and I'll help them. The hard times are not my fault. During these hard times, we'd better face the fact that a family is a team, that there are jobs that have to be done, and that it is no longer important which is men's or women's work. If my wife can get a job these days and I'm laid off, then I'll do my bit with taking care of kids, cleaning the house, and cooking meals. That's man's work, too. It takes a "good man" to be able to do housework when his wife is "bringing home the bacon." It's teamwork that will get us through the hard times. I don't need to feel ashamed. I have to remind myself that the hard times are not my fault.

Not all families will experience job loss or illness, but all families will experience members' growing older over time. Because, however, a system tends toward homeostasis, families may deny these changes. For example, children grow up but the family still treats them as dependent; grandparents grow frail but the family still expects them to be self-sufficient; marriages take place but parents continue to expect the young couple to follow their wishes.

The most vulnerable families, I believe, are the ones that deny change. They are rigid and fragile family systems. Much more research is needed about family denial if we are to understand the ability (and inability) of families to manage stress.

POINTS TO REMEMBER

(1) Denial is a defense mechanism used by family members and families as a whole. Although denial can be viewed as preventing cognitive preparation for an event of family loss, it can be simultaneously viewed as "buying time" so that the family is able to manage that loss. Denial, therefore, is not always resistance as some therapists say. It also may be a way for a family to protect itself while it accepts painful news gradually, bit by bit, as it learns how to manage that news.

(2) In the short term, family denial is functional; in the long term, it is dysfunctional.

(3) Denial most often is found in families in which the stressor situation or event is ambiguous in itself. That is, the family cannot determine clearly if the family member in question is in or out of the family system. In more clearly bounded situations of stress, such as death, family denial is less likely to occur.

(4) To break the family's denial pattern if it has gone on for a long time, family professionals must give members support as well as information to (a) help them to change the situation or, if that is impossible, (b) help them to change their response to the situation. Only after the barrier of denial is broken and the problem is fully recognized and faced can the family begin the process of managing, reorganizing, and moving on to a lower stress level.

FURTHER READING

Armstrong, L. (1979). *Kiss daddy goodnight.* New York: Simon & Schuster.

Black, C. (1981). *It will never happen to me.* Denver, CO: M.A.C. Printing and Publications.

Kübler-Ross, E. (1969). *On death and dying.* New York: Macmillan.

Lindemann, E. (1977). Symptomatology and management of acute grief. In A. Monat & R. S. Lazarus (Eds.), *Stress and coping: An anthology.* New York: Columbia University Press. (Original paper presented at the centenary meeting of the American Psychiatric Association, Philadelphia, May 15-18, 1944)

Miller, A. (1986). *Thou shalt not be aware.* New York: Meridian.

Pearlin, L. I., & Radebaugh, C. W. (1976). Economic strains and the coping functions of alcohol. *American Journal of Sociology, 82,* 652-663.

CHAPTER

6

Family Values
and Belief Systems:

Influences on
Family Stress Management

THE BASIC VALUES OF PEOPLE and the effects of these values on their perceptions and behavior have long been of interest to philosophers and scientists. In 1961, Florence Kluckhohn and Fred Strodtbeck published a study on the nature of value systems and the influence of values on behavior. They field-tested a theory of variation in value orientations in a cross-cultural setting within the United States. The testing took place in the Southwest where, within a radius of 40 miles, five communities that varied culturally were located: a Texan homestead community, a Mormon town, a Spanish-American village, a decentralized Navajo Indian band, and a highly centralized pueblo of Zuni Indians. The field research was carried out during 1950 and 1951. The two researchers measured a person's beliefs on a scale of how the person saw him- or herself in relation to nature. The categories used were (a) subjugation to nature, (b) harmony with nature, and (c) mastery over nature. Each subculture was found to differ.

The Spanish-American subculture valued a subjugation-to-nature orientation. They believed that they could do little or nothing to save land or sheep when storms hit; so they simply accepted the inevitable. Their beliefs about illness and death were as fatalistic as their beliefs about storms and disaster: "If it is the Lord's will that I die, I shall die," and with this belief it was not uncommon for them to refuse medical help (Kluckhohn & Strodtbeck, 1961, p. 13). This orientation was not unlike the Navajo value of "harmony with nature."

On the other hand, the mastery-over-nature orientation was valued by the Texan and Mormon groups; today, it is the predominant orientation of mainstream Americans. The belief is that people can control nature rather than submit to it. We can straighten flooded rivers or build higher bridges. We can build rockets to the moon. The belief that one can control nature, therefore, assumes another value in technology. It is with technology that we shall be able to master and control the problems caused by nature. People who hold this value in mastery and control make statements such as, "God helps those who help themselves." This attitude is very different from the belief that we should not tamper with nature.

WHY VALUES AND BELIEFS MATTER

The reason the study of value orientations is important in the study of family stress is that, even within the United States, families hold different views of stressor events and of how they should respond, depending upon their value orientations. Thus far, this important point has not been incorporated into family stress theory. The omission is critical. We cannot understand *why* some families manage a stressor event and *why* some do not until we take their value orientations into account. A family with a mastery orientation may believe that it can solve anything, and can control just about anything, whatever the event or situation. A family less oriented to mastery may believe in accepting whatever happens to them rather than in trying to remedy or control a situation. Such a family often is described for cultural purposes as "fatalistic."

In the classic definition, fatalism is the belief that everything is determined by a higher power, that all events are predestined and cannot be avoided. In short, fatalism signifies the belief system that whatever happens to a family is predetermined and out of the family's control. Although fatalism is classically defined as believing that volition and effort cannot influence life events, I do not rule out the potential use of volition to lower stress in a situation by a person holding this belief. In my view, however, there is another belief system that opposes mastery but is not so much belief in fatalism as it is acceptance.

From now on when I use the term *fatalism*, I am talking about a family belief system that leans toward the acceptance of situations and events, not because of law or predetermination by a higher power but, primarily, because of cultural and environmental conditioning that reinforces a sense of powerlessness. A better term for the latter belief system would be the German word *Schicksal*; it most accurately represents what I mean by the opposite of a belief in mastery. Like certain definitions of fatalism, Schicksal does not carry with it the implication of predestination; it is simply defined as "this is the way life is." Thus, when I use the English word fatalism, know that I am giving it the German rather than the English definition.

In my observations of families under stress, it has been apparent that the values and beliefs dictating their problem-solving strategies have a cognitive as well as an unconscious component. Even when they are in a hostile environment and are powerless, people and families make choices either to master a situation or to give in to it. Over time they may, in fact, do both. Whenever new information becomes available about an event, however, a major shift may occur in the family's perception of that event and how they will react to it. If a situation is revealed as hopeless, even a mastery-oriented family may shift to a more fatalistic position.

When a family is faced with a problematic event, its beliefs and values determine its action (or lack of it) in the coping process. Indeed, a highly fatalistic value orientation could be a barrier to the coping process because it encourages passivity rather than action; the family would do nothing about the cause of the event on the grounds that the change is controlled by forces outside the family. Individuals might discuss options for changing the event or their perception of it, but intuitively they probably would reject any option. The family's belief system predicts its passive behavior: "We just accept what comes." "We've never been very successful before in coping with problems, so why try now?" "We are losers anyhow, so why fight it?"

The major point that must be kept in mind is that, given the finding in the coping literature that *active* coping strategies are more effective than *passive* strategies, it is logical to assume that families with mastery value orientations will cope with stress more functionally than will families with an orientation toward fatalism (in the sense of Schicksal).

But we must be cautious about this assumption. The following selective review of literature supports such caution. The effectiveness of *action* over *passivity* in coping with stress is situational and may be influenced by larger cultural and contextual variables.

VALUES AND BELIEF AS THEY AFFECT "BLAMING THE VICTIM"

In Western thinking especially, belief in a "just" world is held by many people (Lerner, 1971; Lerner & Simmons, 1966). This belief system values—indeed, requires—control and mastery. According to Festinger

(1957), for us to hold this belief, we must also believe in an objective fit between effort and outcome, and in the availability of this logical fit to all. If this belief in justness and the assumption of its availability to *all* people is accepted, then people in crisis and victims can be viewed as somehow deserving of what they get. If something bad happens to you, it is because you failed somehow. The underlying assumption in this value orientation is that just and "good" people can master and control any event that happens to them and their families. Like the stories of Horatio Alger, Jr., the underlying principle is that hard work and mastery will solve any problem and keep one out of trouble. Nevertheless, sometimes even hardworking people get into trouble. Take the Lynn family, for example.

> Mr. and Mrs. Lynn had a baby that was born defective. Their prayer group said that it was God's way of punishing them for some wrongdoing. So this couple went to extremes to keep the deformed baby at home, feeding it with an eye dropper and being on call at all hours of the day and night. Their other children suffered because the parents were exhausted and guilt-ridden. When the baby finally died a year later, the family was doubly stressed because their prayer group said the baby died because the parents had not been good enough.

> The meaning of the birth and death of this defective baby as defined by the church group influenced the meaning of these events for the family. In this case, the fatalistic orientation was very harmful and blaming, thus increasing the stress level of the family until they were in crisis. In order for the family's stress level to change, the prayer group's perception had to change *or* the family had to separate themselves from that community. Since the former was not possible, they left the prayer group and church and, in fact, moved to a new community. Only then could they change their perception of what had happened to them.

Belief in a just world becomes problematic when we see families who have been just and have done all the right things but, nevertheless, are victimized. If we believe in a fair world but see birth-defective children, for example, we feel discomfort because (a) we can see nothing logical to explain the family's plight and (b) we conclude that if trouble happened illogically to this family, it could also happen to us, no matter how just we are (Watts, 1984).

To believe in a just and logical world is to resist the idea that bad things can happen to good people. Thus we end up blaming the victim. In the case of the Lynn family, their prayer group believed so strongly in a just world that they could only explain the birth of a defective baby as a punishment from God upon the unworthy parents. The prayer group could *not* see that sometimes bad things happen to good people and that life is not always fair.

Given such beliefs and attitudes, coping behaviors are necessarily influenced. We deny a person's affliction because it is illogical or, as the prayer group did, we fabricate a logical reason to explain what we see. We protect ourselves by believing that bad things happen *only* to bad people. Too often, we may conclude that because a family was once in trouble, it is no wonder that they are in more trouble or that they are poor and on welfare, generation after generation. We blame the victim as we struggle to explain why bad things happen to good people. Because we are the people of Western culture who value mastery, we struggle to find a logic in what happens to us, often to the detriment of families who already are badly stressed.

People from Eastern cultures that are more fatalistically oriented can more easily tolerate the illogical. They may attribute the misfortune of a defective baby to fate *without* moral judgment on justness or unjustness. Easterners more readily than Westerners accept the fact that the world is not always fair and logical. They do not judge that fact in terms of good or bad. It simply is the way life is.

In order to understand the meaning of a stressful event for a family and to assess their subsequent management strategies, researchers and therapists must first determine the family's beliefs and value orientation. Certainly, a family's value of mastery is a relevant influence on their perception of troublesome events and their decision on how to deal with the problem.

The idea of mastery and a just world can also be found in the military. It is reported that combat soldiers in Vietnam took seriously the old army adage that "if you do your job right, you'll stay out of trouble" (Bourne, 1969, p. 108). Soldiers defended themselves with this belief and it appeared to be effective in allowing them to deal with the threat of death in combat. They reported that their fears of death were overshadowed by feelings of invulnerability and the belief that if they performed with the skill and action in which they had been trained, they would be safe from harm (Bourne, 1969). It appears, then, that even the fear of death can be assuaged by the combination of (a) denial of the threat of death and (b) reliance on one's skills. Together, they are effective coping strategies not only for soldiers in Vietnam but also for people facing overwhelming odds, as in the treatment of cancer or AIDS. Some believe they actually can control the disease. There is growing evidence that it may be possible in some cases.

On the other hand, during the Holocaust, many Jews valued their traditional fatalistic passivity over mastery to cope with the Nazi threat of death. (The participants in the Warsaw ghetto uprising were a notable exception.) According to Hilberg (1961), a historian of the

Holocaust, the two basic coping patterns used by many Jews during that period were (a) an attempt to avert action and, if that failed, (b) automatic compliance with the enemy. Coping patterns were based on what the Jewish culture had learned over the ages, that "in order to survive, they had to refrain from resistance" (p. 666). Hence, according to Hilberg, their coping strategies of cooperation and submission were based on repression and denial. For example, in the recorded minutes of the 1941 Viennese Jewish Conference of War Invalids, direct reference to death was obviously avoided. The Jewish war invalids wrote only of seeing "black" and of "tempting fate" (Hilberg, 1961, p. 668) with no mention of death or threat of annihilation. Perhaps passivity and denial are the only coping strategies available to victimized families who see discrimination and maltreatment as their heritage and fate. This belief gives victimized people a perception that they can do nothing about their situation no matter how painful and life-threatening it is. A fatalistic value orientation goes hand in hand with the feeling of powerlessness. Indeed, in the face of overwhelming odds passivity sometimes may preserve lives.

During the Vietnam conflict, prisoners of war also used submission as a coping mechanism. In order to minimize torture or the threat of death, they reported using a passive model of adaptation. For example, they internalized anger and did not act it out directly in front of their captors (Hall & Malone, 1974; McCubbin, 1979). In 1980, some Iranian hostages used passive measures to survive their captivity, for example, reading, being quiet, and sleeping a lot. At the same time, other hostages used more active coping strategies, such as yelling at and cursing their captors or making messes for them to clean up (personal communications, 1982).

In 1980, the Disaster Section of the National Institute of Mental Health sponsored a study on the importance of value orientations in response to family stress and coping. The principal investigator, Ron Nuttal, investigated family coping in American communities that were struck by four different types of natural disaster: (a) the loss of kin due to the breaking of a dam, (b) the loss of property in a flood in Johnstown, Pennsylvania, (c) the effects of a nonviolent disaster (a blizzard) in Buffalo, New York, and (d) the coastal flooding of three towns in Massachusetts after a seawall caved in. From this diverse research pool, Nuttal (1980) identified *verstehen* ("understanding the meaning") as a significant variable in explaining family stress. His major finding was that the unique *meaning* of the event for *each* community was a critical variable. Note that the communities were all within the United States. When a flood was perceived fatalistically by a community as a message from God, the meaning and subsequent coping strategies were different from those used when the flood was viewed as a failure of mastery through technology. Families with a fatalistic belief system coped more passively in the belief that nothing could be done about the possible destruction. Rather than move away or build houses on stilts, these families just accepted the destruction and cleaned up in its wake. On the other hand, more mastery-oriented families coped actively by building a dam, moving away, or building a house on stilts. These families did not passively accept the destruction but used technology and their own efforts to manage and control the event.

Following Nuttal's exploratory study, C. Kagitcibasi (1983), a Turkish sociologist, investigated how Turkish families coped with the disaster of earthquakes and floods. She provided support for the premise that a cultural value of fatalism affects a family's response to disaster. She went on to identify the fatalistic belief system as interfering with social change; people who believed in fatalism would not move or relocate *even in the face of disaster*. The fatalistic beliefs of Turkish peasants are well-documented (e.g., Frey, 1963; Kagitcibasi, 1983). In addition, Kagitcibasi concluded that fatalistic (high external) locus-of-control tendencies are prevalent among people who are more often *victims* of natural disasters: the urban poor and rural peasants; they tend to perceive natural disasters as inevitable and as bad fortune that have to be endured due to overpowering mystical and supernatural forces.

Like Kluckhohn, Strodtbeck, and Nuttal, Kagitcibasi made a strong case for cultural variation in the qualitative meaning of disastrous events for Turkish peasants. She hypothesized, however, that a fatalistic value orientation may be *functional* for Turkish rural peasants and urban poor when they lack access to technology that could predict and control disastrous events, and when they do not have the economic means to acquire protection or to move to a safer place. In short, in situations in which families have few resources and alternatives, they can cope only by passively accepting what comes their way and resigning themselves to "God's will"; such resignation actually may "provide psychological relief and social solidarity" through strengthening a sense of community belongingness (Kagitcibasi, 1983, p. 78).

Nevertheless, passive belief systems negate the likelihood of social change and *support the status quo* of families in dire stress and hardship. Like the fate of Jews during the Holocaust and families in cycles of poverty, passive acceptance in the long run may be destructive.

Therefore it is apparent that a fatalistic belief system may be functional *only when nothing can be done to change the situation* that is producing stress. By their very nature the values of fatalism versus mastery are highly related to the values of status quo as opposed to change. A family's cultural context, which comes from the larger cultural context and the community, and its belief system control its assessment of the event and the selection of passive or active coping strategies. The cultural linkage must be taken into account.

The problematic question raised by the Turkish research just cited is whether the belief system influences the inability to cope actively with the stressor event *or* whether the lack of resources to cope actively with the event fosters a fatalistic belief system as a passive adaptation. Which came first: fatalistic beliefs or a lack of resources? Which is cause and which is effect? Because of this question, family researchers, therapists, and educators need to determine not only the cultural value orientation but also the relation of the value orientation to the stressful event or situation: Is the value orientation blocking the stress management process and thereby reinforcing a status quo that may harm the family and its members? If a family stays on the banks of a flooding river long enough, their resources to cope and manage eventually will be depleted. Ultimately, passive acceptance no longer will be life enhancing. The family's passive acceptance may make their stress less painful psychologically but it will not halt or reverse the process of destruction and crisis. Only active behaviors will change the direction of that process.

To further complicate the picture, structural as well as perceptual constraints result from the cultural context. For example, it may be impossible for some families to move to high ground or to resist impending doom even if they wanted to because of scarce economic resources or membership in the wrong caste. If only rich people hold the higher ground or if only upper classes are to be spared from death camps, then the remaining individuals or families have no choice of coping strategy. Those who remain in the path of disaster may have to use acceptance as a coping strategy because, given cultural restraints, they have no control over making changes. The poor and lower classes, because of their lack of resources and power, often are unable to manage stressful events well, and, thus remain highly vulnerable as they depend on the coping strategies of passive acceptance or fatalism simply because *these are all they have.*

The attribution of stress outcomes to cultural belief systems and values was documented by two American researchers, Feldman and

McCarthy (1983), in their study of the disaster of famine and its relation to cultural attitudes and macroeconomics in Bangladesh. The attribution of the outcome of the family stress process to cultural belief systems was also documented by Kagitcibasi (1983) in her Turkish research. Famine among poor people and the macroeconomics of the larger cultural context are highly interrelated. This relation held true more recently in Africa also.

VALUES, STRESS MANAGEMENT, AND GENDER: ARE THEY RELATED?

From the preceding selective review of research, it can be concluded that passive acceptance is functional at some times in order to cope with a stressor event, but dysfunctional at other times. That is, "flowing with the tide" and giving up efforts to take control sometimes lowers stress. Nevertheless, there are times when one must help oneself, when one must act and take charge of a situation in order to reduce stress levels. Ultimately, lowering the level of stress is what matters, not the value orientation leading to that outcome. Sometimes being active is functional in the management of stress but being passive is the only way for a family to manage at other times.

Essentially, we must still investigate and document more about *when* it is functional to be active and controlling and *when* it is functional to be more passive and resigned. In mainstream America, a mastery orientation is valued. Research also indicates active coping behaviors are more functional than passive behaviors. There may therefore be gender differences in how stress as well as coping are viewed.

McFarlane and Sussman (1982), in their research on family mobility, determined that "sources of stress during a move are attributed to *external* and *uncontrollable* factors" (p. 9), but all family members do not necessarily name the same factors. Wives tended to define moving as stressful *if it affected family relationships*, whereas husbands classified moving as stressful *if they did not want to make the move*; that is, if the impetus for the move was out of their control.

On the basis of early clinical observations, it appears that women as caregivers operate differently than do male caregivers. As Carol Gilligan (1985) writes in her recent book, males and females may approach problem solving "in a different voice." Given that Alzheimer caregivers are usually of an older age, we can assume a more traditional socialization regarding gender roles: men as instrumental, in charge, and active; women as expressive, supportive, and more passive.

Such socialization will, I propose, have a major effect on how the caregiver perceives and responds to the event of chronic illness, in this case Alzheimer's disease. For example, a woman caregiver stopped going to church, her primary social support, only because she believed she could not go without her husband. She felt her place as a wife was with him. She would not, even for the sake of her own health, violate this traditional belief in "a woman's role." Another woman stopped taking her blood pressure pills because the medication made her too tired to care for her bedridden husband. Only when concerned relatives intervened did she take care of her own needs and reluctantly allow them to institutionalize her husband.

On the other hand, a male caregiver was without guilt when he said he still kept his bowling dates because he knew he had to do so to keep from going crazy. He used respite care at least once a week because he knew he had to get out in spite of his devotion to his totally bedridden wife. This same male caregiver, when asked what helped him the most with his stress, immediately replied, "The Hoyer lift," a steel lift that made it less painful for his wife to be lifted from bed to wheelchair and back again. He also showed us wool pads and other items of technology that made his life easier because, he said, they eased her pain.

When another woman caregiver was asked what made her life less stressful, she answered, "romance novels." Her coping mechanism was, stereotypically for her gender, more passive; her male counterpart's coping mechanisms were stereotypically more active and technology oriented.

In light of these early findings, I propose that rigid traditional role socialization is a barrier to stress management. Given that loss is a certainty in family life, I propose that gender socialization needs to be less rigid for both males and females. Much more research needs to be done regarding gender differences in family stress management.

If caregivers value mastery over fatalism, action over passivity, or control over acceptance for the way things are, that will make a difference in how they perceive and deal with the event of loss. I predict that those who have more resources will be more mastery oriented and will rely more heavily on technology to solve their problems. They will rely more heavily on self-help information than on groups in which feelings are shared. They want information so that they can act to solve problems and reduce stress. Research indicates that people in Western cultures are more mastery oriented than people in Eastern cultures but, more specifically, that the rich more than the poor and the male more than the female are mastery oriented in their approach to lowering stress. The value of mastery is, of course, related to the selection of

"LOOK HONEY, I JUST BOUGHT THE ANSWER TO ALL OF OUR PROBLEMS!"

Figure 6.1

active coping strategies such as those described above (i.e., the male caregiver using respite care so he could continue bowling).

Passive coping strategies, on the other hand, are found in people who have a more fatalistic orientation. Because of their value orientation, they need less to be in control and can better accept the way things are. Such people are less likely to set limits on demands on their time because they believe a higher power will take care of them. In the classic chicken-and-egg argument, however, it is not certain whether the passive, fatalistic orientation is the cause or the result of being poor and having fewer resources. It may be that economic status is a primary predictor of value orientation. The passive, fatalistic belief system may result from the family learning they have no resources or power to change a situation. Having an incurable illness may be just such a situation of powerlessness.

At any rate, determining the belief system of a caregiver will, I believe, be paramount in determining, first, how the caregiver perceives the event of Alzheimer's disease in their family and, second, how he or she will cope with it. Finally, it will determine what kind of support or information the caregiver will accept to ease their own stress with this chronic situation.

POINTS TO REMEMBER

(1) Family values and beliefs may predict their vulnerability to stress and how they go about managing stress levels.

(2) Because family belief systems and value orientations will influence how families perceive stressor events and how they cope with, manage, or solve problems, the levels of stress stimulated by a particular stressor event will vary across religions, subcultures, and cultures.

(3) The more fatalistically oriented the family's belief system, the more *passive* they will be in their management of stress; the more mastery-oriented the family's belief system, the more *active* they will become in their management of stress. Although value orientation and belief systems have their source in the larger culture (external context), there appear to be differences in the shaping of values and beliefs between families, even within a community, and within families. Because of this malleability, values and beliefs are part of the family's internal context.

(4) Family belief systems may exhibit gender differences. Research has only recently begun to look at those important differences.

(5) Although a fatalistic belief system may be functional in the short run when a disastrous event strikes and nothing can be done to reverse it, that same belief system may be dysfunctional in the long run because *it will interfere with social change*. If a person clings to the belief that an event is the result of fate, Karma, God's will, or some other higher power, it will block the process that can *change* the situation, *change* the use of resources, or *change* the perception of what is occurring. Believing that one has mastery over a situation aids the process of developing *active* behaviors to manage the event or stimulate a revolution in the family that will change the family's perception of reality and, thereby, their way of managing stress. If a person believes in a just world and values mastery, he or she may also believe it is not logical for bad things to happen to good people and will therefore blame the victim.

(6) If the situation is hopeless, loss inevitable, and control impossible, the more mastery-oriented families will be more likely to fall into crisis than will the more fatalistically oriented families. On the other hand, a family with a strong value of mastery may be less likely to give up hope even in what is a hopeless situation, such as terminal illness of a family member or loss of a family farm.

(7) In situations of chronic, long-term family illness, the value orientation of fatalism may be dysfunctional in that it prevents systemic change. The family tries to pretend that nothing has changed or that there is nothing they can do to help themselves. Because of their passivity, the system will remain in high stress.

(8) A family's value orientation must be determined before we can understand *why* families manage or fail to manage stress.

FURTHER READING

Arsenian, J., & Arsenian, J. M. (1948). Tough and easy cultures: A conceptual analysis. *Psychiatry, 11*, 377-385.

Bianco, C. (1974). *The two rosetos.* Bloomington: Indiana University Press.

Bolin, R. C., & Bolton, P. A. (1983). Recovery in Nicaragua and the U.S.A. In O. Hultaker & J. Trost (Eds.), *International Journal of Mass Emergencies and Disasters, 1*(1), 125-144.

Boss, P., & Weiner, J. P. (1988). Rethinking assumptions about women, development, and family therapy. In C. J. Falicov (Ed.), *Family transitions: Continuity and change over the life cycle.* New York: Guilford Press.

Bruhn, J. G., Chandler, B., Miller, M. C., Wolf, S., & Lynn, T. N. (1966). Social aspects of coronary heart disease in two adjacent ethnically different communities. *American Journal of Public Health, 56*, 1493-1506.

Caplan, G. (1964). *Principles of preventive psychiatry.* New York: Basic Books.

Caplan, G. (1981). Mastery and stress: Psychological aspects. *American Journal of Psychiatry, 138*(4), 413-420.

Feldman, S., & McCarthy, F. E. (1982). National trends affecting disaster response and family organization in Bangladesh. In O. Hultaker & J. Trost (Eds.), *International Journal of Mass Emergencies and Disasters.* Sweden: International University Library Press.

Feldman, S., & McCarthy, F. E. (1983). Disaster response in Bangladesh. In O. Hultaker & J. Trost (Eds.), *International Journal of Mass Emergencies and Disasters, 1*(1), 105-124.

Frey, F. W. (1963). Surveying peasant attitudes in Turkey. *Public Opinion Quarterly, 27*, 335-355.

Gilligan, C. (1985). *In a different voice.* Cambridge, MA: Harvard University Press.

Kagitcibasi, C. (1983). How does the traditional family in Turkey cope with disasters? In O. Hultaker & J. Trost (Eds.), *International Journal of Mass Emergencies and Disasters, 1*(1), 145-152.

Kluckhohn, F. R., & Strodtbeck, F. L. (1961). *Variations in value orientation.* Westport, CT: Greenwood Press.

Moos, R. H., Finney, J., & Chan, D. (1981). The process of recovery from alcoholism: Comparing alcoholic patients and matched community controls. *Journal of Studies on Alcohol, 42*, 383-402.

Nuttal, R. L. (1980). *Coping with catastrophe: Family adjustments to national disaster.* Keynote address presented at Groves Conference on Marriage and the Family, Gatlinburg, TN.

Pearlin, L. I., & Leiberman, M. A. (1979). Social sources of emotional distress. In R. G. Simmons (Ed.), *Research in community mental health.* Greenwich, CT: JAI Press.

Reiss, D. (1981). *The family's construction of reality.* Cambridge, MA: Harvard University Press.

Sontag, S. (1979). *Illness as metaphor.* New York: Random House.

Weiner, J. P., & Boss, P. (1985). Exploring gender bias against women: Ethics for marriage and family therapy [Special issue]. *Counseling and Values.*

CHAPTER

7

The Family's External Context

GLOBAL PRESSURES AFFECT FAMILY STRESS. Distance has been shrunk by almost instantaneous communication. Threat of nuclear accidents, environmental pollution, economic uncertainty, terrorism, mass starvation, and space accidents, for example, are brought into homes by instantaneous communication. We are made immediately aware of tragedies and events over which we have no control (except to turn off the television set). More than ever, family stress is influenced by external events because we are now made witness to them; yet we cannot control them. The development of agriculture and industry in underdeveloped countries, for example, has led to the decline of jobs for factory workers and family farmers in the United States. Many of the problems that families in the United States face today are global in origin, and the family has little power to affect global change.

For those acculturated to be mastery oriented, to solve problems, and to work their own way out of difficulties, the constraints imposed by such external forces leave them bewildered and angry. Added are the frustrations imposed by local communities (e.g., getting caught in traffic jams, waiting at airports, standing in long lines for unemployment checks, rising rents, and tax increases). It is no wonder then that many families today live with a higher level of stress than did those in previous generations. In American society, one that by world standards is highly developed, high stress may be attributable less to a lack of family resources than to a conflict between acculturation for mastery and the restraints imposed upon families by conditions they cannot control. The ratio of control to restraints may therefore predict how well a family will manage stress.

THE FORCES WITH WHICH FAMILIES CONTEND

The question asked at the beginning of this book was *why* are some families vulnerable to crisis and others not. I have proposed in preceding chapters that the answer lies in the meaning an event holds for a specific family and for the individuals in it. Of all the factors that Reuben Hill originally related to crisis (A, B, C, and X), I have in this book focused on the C factor, the family's perception of the stressor event or situation, as a major determinant of outcome. The family's ability to manage stress may depend more on perception than on resources. In the studies of boundary ambiguity, this premise has been supported.

Perception, although psychological in origin and, thus, under the control of individuals and families, is mediated by the larger context in which a stress event takes place. In Chapters 4, 5, and 6, I discussed the effects of the internal context on perception in relation to family boundary ambiguity, the use of denial, and value orientation. Here I examine how the context *external* to the family affects the family's perception and therefore influences the management of stress.

Figures 2.1 and 2.2 show the five dimensions of the external context: history, economics, development, heredity, and culture. Each was defined in Chapter 2; more general discussions are presented here. Ideas are presented so that they can be tested since little research is available on family stress from the perspective of external constraints.

History

The time at which a stressor event takes place in a family impinges on how the family manages the resultant stress. Contextual time markers leave their traces on family stress through a ripple effect (like a stone tossed into water) from the societal out to the family level. A Vietnam veteran may have a marriage problem, but to deal with it the couple must resolve their separate Vietnam experiences: namely, the vet's in the war itself and the spouse's, at home. The same is true for the participants in the fight for civil rights. When the movement for equal rights started at the societal level, it was inevitable that the philosophy would begin to be reflected in marriages. In short, a family's historical context intrudes on its perceptions.

Economics

The management of stress within a family is often complicated by the condition of the state's or nation's economy that influences the family's income. For example, losing a job may mean the cancellation of medical and hospital insurance at a time when a family member finds she is pregnant. The loss of the job would be less stressful under these circumstances if the family were to acquire a sudden windfall (e.g., a substantial prize in a state-run lottery or stock market gains) but more stressful if real estate taxes were to rise precipitously. In recent years, American farm families have suffered because foreign markets for their crops and products have diminished; however hard the family farmers may work, they still are on the brink of failure because of global economic manipulations.

Development

Historical and economic dimensions sometimes overlap developmental dimensions, which constrains the family stress management process. As stated in Chapter 2, development is included in the external context because it is something the family *cannot control*; maturation is a process controlled by biology. For example, children grow up and leave home, but the drop in university and college admissions during the economic recession of the early 1980s suggests that many high school graduates were forced to give up their dreams of a college degree to look for work. And when no jobs were available, the young people continued to live at home instead of becoming independent. Historical, economic, and developmental dimensions now intersected to interrupt the usual process, and tension was likely to be at a higher level.

Other developmental milestones also create and exacerbate family stress. For example, having aged parents is likely to be more stressful today now that technology has made it possible for people to live longer. Unfortunately, family and societal policies have not yet adapted to this new longevity. Today's population boom is in the "over 65" category. We have been socialized to believe that our parents must care for us when we are young; but no one prepares us for the possibility of our having to care for parents when they are old. Nor does the social system provide us adequately with resources to look after the elderly in our homes if we so choose.

Aging is a developmental context that interacts with the current historical context of medical breakthroughs to increase life spans and the populations of the elderly. Increased longevity becomes stressful for adult children when their elderly parent is chronically ill and frail. Unfortunately, this burden continues to fall predominantly on adult daughters rather than sons. The increased stress this presents for the middle generation, who may be launching adolescents, supporting adult children, or even preparing for retirement themselves places them in a generational squeeze. With pressure coming from both above and below, they have been called the "sandwich generation." Midlife families, and especially midlife women, are now considered high risk because of simultaneous stress stemming from the need of elderly parents, launching children, housework, employment demands, and their own retirement plans. (For further discussions on gender and development, see Gilligan, 1985, 1986, who suggests that gender differences in development may reflect the interaction of universal human experience with a larger political context. This is new information and will have a major impact on redefining the family developmental context.)

Heredity

The biological and genetic makeup of the family is also placed external to the family, and for the same reason: The family has no control over it. Some people, and therefore families, are simply stronger than others because of their genes. We talk of aged people who have lived long despite hard lives as "coming from good stock." One surely can say that George Burns, who is still on stage at 91, has a good heredity. People like him seem to have more of the stamina, resilience, energy, and perseverance that are needed to activate and maintain the stress management process. A good constitution simply makes it easier to defend oneself and one's family when a stressor event occurs.

Culture

Finally, the *cultural* context is a major part of the external context in that it provides the canons and rules to which families react and by which they define events of stress. For example, when the culture supports the denial of a physical loss, the family system has great difficulty in grieving and closing out the missing member. Let me illustrate this point.

In Ireland, divorce is not yet permitted or recognized; thus desertion is the only culturally acceptable way for a husband and wife to separate. The deserted family, however, has an uncertain legal status; the uncertainty, in turn, fosters ambiguity and, thus, high stress. An abandoned wife cannot close out her missing husband and start anew, reorganizing as either a single parent or someone else's wife (which she might do if divorce were permitted). She remains technically and legally a "deserted wife"; the government recognizes this ambiguous state by providing pensions to support her and her family. In its zeal to protect intact families (by outlawing divorce), the government blocks the families from initiating the restructuring processes that normally would take place after a husband (or wife) walks out. These families cannot clarify their boundaries because the law will not permit it. They are held in limbo by the culture and the state.

In Judaism, similar laws block change after a husband has disappeared. For example, because death cannot be presumed, even after a lapse of time, and a missing husband cannot deliver a *get* (his consent to divorce), the wife, who may in fact be a widow, is barred forever from remarriage (Wegner, 1982, p. 182).

Another example of the external culture influencing the family's internal context, specifically boundary ambiguity, is also found in Judaism; it involves the status of stillborn babies. Mourning rites are accorded only viable babies. Thus the family of a stillborn baby does not collectively grieve the loss by gathering and sitting *shiva* for the traditional seven days, which is the cultural practice upon the death of viable family members. The stillborn is taken from the mother and buried without a headstone or ceremony, thereby denying her and her husband the right and the support to grieve openly. By giving the stillborn baby the status of "nonperson," the culture denies the loss. Perhaps in Biblical times, when nomads roamed the Near East, such a restriction may have been necessary to protect individuals from falling behind and becoming prey to enemies. But continuance of such restrictions today, in Judaic as well as non-Judaic cultures, means that a woman is culturally pressured to deny the biological fact that she had nurtured a potential life inside her body. The denial of the experience by not mourning the miscarried fetus or stillborn child creates a situation of high boundary ambiguity that may interfere with the competent functioning of the family well into the future.

Families who belong to a subculture (e.g., military, foreign service, or ethnic) often find themselves in conflict with the mainstream culture. The Native American subculture, for example, values consensus and collective decision making, whereas American culture as a whole values independence, self-sufficiency, and competition. The values of the family's internal context, hence, are in direct conflict with the values of the external context. The cultural incongruence between internal and external contexts may help to answer the question of why some ethnic minority families are especially stressed and often in crisis. The same kind of conflict may help to explain the stress of women in some

families. In the wider culture, gender roles are prescribed by custom
and expectations: what it means to be a girl or a boy, a man or a woman,
a husband or a wife. The differences become important in family stress
management.

In earlier chapters, I established that active rather than passive
coping behaviors are more functional in family stress management. In
American culture, male children are nurtured to take action to solve
problems and to care for themselves. The problem is that many
females, especially those who are the parents of adult children, were
socialized to be *passive*, not active. When young, we were told that
"girls look pretty" or that "nice girls don't sweat." Fairy tales like "Snow
White" and "Sleeping Beauty," in which good women remained passive
until a handsome prince rescued them, were our social models
(Bernard, 1972; Bettelheim, 1977; DeBeauvoir, 1953; Dowling, 1981;
French, 1977; Friedan, 1963; Kolbenschlag, 1979). The only strong
women in the fairy tales were witches or wicked stepmothers, and one
did not want to be like them.

Even as late as the 1950s, young women were socialized to believe
that passivity was feminine and active and masterful behaviors were
reserved for men. This kind of upbringing is detrimental not only to
women's and girls' abilities to cope with stress but also to the
psychological development of some boys. If women are socialized to be
passive, to not make waves, to trust in destiny, they will not be able to
manage stress well. A battered woman will wait to be rescued rather
than take the initiative to protect herself by escaping to a shelter or
calling the police. A woman who is divorced, widowed, or a single
parent often waits for a "Prince Charming" to rescue her. However, if
no prince comes along, most single women learn to become self-
sufficient in most areas of life. Unfortunately, single women, especially
those who are old and alone, are frequently victimized financially.

This enculturation, I believe, has been detrimental primarily to
women and girls; it can also be harmful to men and boys, however, if
cultural rules lead them to believe that they must always master
problems and must never give in. How stressful this attitude is for males
who face an event that cannot be solved, for example, a terminal illness,
the loss of the family farm, or a big bully on the playground! Having been
taught that they must always win, men and boys have a more difficult
time accepting loss than individuals who, by culture, are more passive
and fatalistic.

What is evident—I speak here on the basis of my research and of
therapy sessions with stressed families—is the following: *both* active
and passive coping strategies are necessary for *both* males and females
if they are to be good at managing family stress.[1]

SOCIETAL PRESSURE ON THE FAMILY

Although the external context is presented in this book as a restraint on families, family professionals, policymakers, and researchers must help families work for change in this larger arena if family stress is to be eased in this era. Societies expect the family to be their keystone, but most do little to strengthen the family for that role. The increasing pressures of the world cannot be tranquilized by the family. That is not a realistic expectation.

The family must become more than a passive reactor to cultural demands. Families can find their own solutions to managing troubles and pressures (as did Inez Moore's family, described in Chapter 1), and they must be supported to do so. Families must be active and not just passive in relation to external demands and restraints. To carry out this goal, families will require support and expertise from family scientists, marriage and family therapists, family life educators, family medicine specialists, family lawyers, and family policymakers. None can work with the family without considering the external context.

POINTS TO REMEMBER

(1) The family's perception of a stressor event is mediated by the external context.

(2) The external context is composed of five dimensions: time in history, macroeconomics, human development, heredity, and culture. These dimensions are imposed upon the family; the family has no control over them. Thus the external context is composed of restraints within which the family must manage its stress.

(3) More than in previous generations, global pressures affect family stress. Through mass media, families are made aware of global events that affect them but that they cannot control. This adds to family stress.

(4) The balance of acculturation for mastery balanced with external constraints placed on the family may predict how well a family can manage stress.

(5) Gender issues originating in the larger culture may increase family vulnerability to stress.

(6) Although the external context is presented as constraining to families, it is for family professionals and policymakers to help families work for change in this larger arena. We cannot separate the external context from our work with families. That view would be too myopic.

NOTE

1. The Serenity Prayer written by St. Francis of Assisi represents an attitude toward family stress management that has proven helpful to both men and women in stress for many generations: "God grant me the serenity to accept the things I cannot change, courage to change those things I can, and wisdom to know the difference." People from many Eastern and Western cultures have found this approach to stress management useful.

FURTHER READING

Bartlett, G. S., Houts, P. S., Byrnes, L. K., & Miller, R. W. (1983). The near disaster at Three Mile Island. In O. Hultaker & J. Trost (Eds.), *International Journal of Mass Emergencies and Disasters, 1*(1), 19-42.

Brubaker, T. (1985). *Later life families*. Beverly Hills, CA: Sage.

Carter, E., & McGoldrick, M. (1980). *The family life cycle: A framework for family therapy*. New York: Gardner Press.

Elder, G. H. (1974). *Children of the Great Depression*. Chicago: University of Chicago Press.

Elder, G. H., & Rockwell, R. C. (1979). The life-course and human development: An ecological perspective. *International Journal of Behavioral Development, 2*, 1-21.

Erickson, E. (1950). *Childhood and society*. New York: W. W. Norton.

Gilligan, C. (1986). Exit-voice dilemmas in adolescent development. In A. Foxley, M. McPherson, & G. O'Donnell (Eds.), *Development, democracy, and the art of trespassing: Essays in honor of Albert O. Hirschman*. Notre Dame, IN: University of Notre Dame Press.

Guntern, G. (1979). *Social change, stress and mental health in the pearl of the Alps*. New York: Springer-Verlag.

Henry, J. P., & Stephen, P. M. (1977). *Stress, health and the social environment: A sociobiologic approach to medicine*. New York: Springer-Verlag.

Insel, P. M., & Moos, R. H. (Eds.). (1974). *Health and the social environment*. Lexington, MA: Lexington Books.

Kellam, S. G., Ensminger, M. E., & Turner, R. J. (1977). Family structure and the mental health of children. *Archives of General Psychiatry, 34*, 1012-1022.

Kiritz, S., & Moos, R. H. (1974). Psychological effects of social environments. *Psychosomatic Medicine, 36*, 96-114.

Lieberman, E. (1971). American families and the Vietnam War. *Journal of Marriage and the Family, 33*, 709-721.

Melson, G. F. (1980). *Family and environment: An ecosystem perspective*. Minneapolis: Burgess.

Palgi, P. (1970). The adaptability and vulnerability of family types in the changing Israeli society. In A. Jarvus & J. Marcus (Eds.), *Children and families in Israel*. New York: Gordon & Breech.

Palgi, P. (1973). Socio-cultural expressions and implications of death, mourning, and bereavement. In *Israel arising out of the war situation*. Israel: Jerusalem Academic Press.

Palgi, P. (1975). *Culture and mourning: Expressions of bereavement arising out of the war situation in Israel*. Paper presented at the International Conference on Psychological Stress and Adjustment in Time of War and Peace, Tel Aviv, Israel.

Walker, A. (1985). Reconceptualizing family stress. *Journal of Marriage and the Family, 47*(4), 827-837.

CHAPTER
8

Victimization and Family Crisis[1]

THE FATHER OF ONE OF THE ASTRONAUTS killed in the *Challenger* space shuttle disaster in 1986 said of NASA, "They have forgotten that there are mothers and fathers of the victims."[2] He was right. There always are two sets of victims in a disaster; those directly involved and those waiting at home.[3]

Theories of victimization have developed out of research on the effects of war, specifically the Holocaust of World War II and then the Vietnam War. More recently, feminists have broadened the theory to include victimization of women. Victims of rape and war have something in common: both are rendered helpless, both have lost self-esteem, and both no longer trust the world as fair and just (see Danieli, 1985; Figley, 1978, 1985; Janoff-Bulman & Frieze, 1983).

Now that we recognize that families as well as individuals can be victims, there is a need to develop theory for family victimization. If we cannot understand how the crisis of victimization happens to families, then we cannot help them to recover. In order to reach for family strength and empowerment, we must first understand family helplessness and victimization. In this chapter, I begin to develop theoretical ideas to help reach this goal.

Victimization is the overpowering of a person or family with physical or psychological trauma that results in feelings of helplessness, distrust, and shame. To be victimized, loss must occur: loss of power, loss of control over what is happening, and, most debilitating, loss of self-esteem. The family therefore loses not only an object or person, but they also lose their pride and confidence as a team. They feel shamed. (For a detailed discussion of shame from a family systems perspective, see Fossum & Mason, 1986.)

A catastrophic event or situation is the prerequisite for the trauma. It may be a deliberate cruelty (e.g., terrorism) or a natural disaster (e.g., an earthquake or flood); it could be a human-made catastrophe (e.g., the 1986 nuclear energy malfunction at Chernobyl in the Soviet Union) or a calamity triggered by an event inside the family (e.g., a hopeless, chronic disease or an abusive pattern of interaction).

When a person is so traumatized, whether taken hostage, terrorized, kidnapped, raped, abused, or tortured, both the individual and the family who cares about him or her are immobilized. The family does not know where their loved one is, whether he or she is dead or alive, whether they will ever see this family member again, and whether they can do anything to help change the situation. If they are dealing with an unfamiliar culture, which happens frequently today, the family does not understand the logic of the situation. For both family and victim, belief in a just world is shattered by such catastrophes. Nothing makes sense in a rape or a mugging. Certainly there is not much sense in waging a war for pieces of jungle or in the taking of innocent hostages by terrorists. And nothing makes sense in the beating of a baby by an enraged father or the sexual abuse of young boys and girls by the very people who should be protecting them.

FAMILY VICTIMIZATION AS CRISIS

In Figure 8.1, I classify and illustrate victimization as a crisis. Victimization is an example of crisis because the person and family are immobilized. They are trapped, cornered or overpowered, physically or psychologically, and they cannot function. During the Iranian hostage crisis, a little country held a big country hostage. We were powerless and shamed by our inability to act. The yellow ribbons displayed all over the country became a form of catharsis that alleviated somewhat our feeling of impotence. We wanted to fight back; to show the Iranian terrorists that they could not bully us. Had we won a battle to free the hostages, however, they might have been killed. So America, a superpower, was immobilized. And because our American heritage of mastery was not appeased by President Carter's quiet negotiation, we voted him out of office.

Victimization works best when the perpetrator produces that sense of immobilization and helplessness plus a loss of self-respect. This is true within the family as well as in world politics. With rape, violence, incest, and abuse of the young or aged, there must be a power differential for the trauma to occur. Someone must be aggressive and

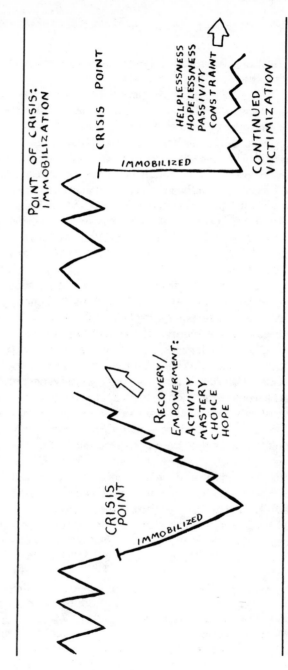

Figure 8.1: Victimization as Crisis

another person must be made to feel helpless. Humiliation helps bring about the helplessness.

Charles Figley (1985), a family psychologist who has studied victimization extensively, rates family abuse as the most debilitating of all forms. The reason is that the source of comfort is, at the same time, the source of pain. But families also can be victimized by situations outside their internal boundaries. Survivors of the Nazi Holocaust still suffer the effects of their victimization as shown by the pain, distrust, survivor guilt, and shame for their passivity that they have passed down to their descendants. Danieli (1985) calls this "the intergenerational transmission of victimization" (1985, p. 295). For both families and individuals, the transmission of victimization can be stopped by (a) redefining the event, (b) finding some meaning in the terrible thing that happened, (c) changing one's behaviors to prevent its happening again, (d) seeking social support, especially from people who successfully coped with a similar event, and (e) focusing on self-blame regarding their behavior (see next section for explanation).

Some families victimize internally (father is incestuous, mother does not stop him) and other families are victimized externally (by war, discrimination, terrorism). Whenever there is a victim, there is a victimized family. Families of the 1,258 men still missing in action in Southeast Asia would agree, and so too would the families of hostages taken by terrorists and of children kidnapped by angry parents. Certainly, the families of soldiers who returned from the jungles of Vietnam would agree, for they were victimized also by American public attitudes toward them.

When individuals have experienced traumatic events, it is now established that the effects can become or can even reoccur at a later time (delayed). The American Psychiatric Association in their diagnostic manual has labeled this "post traumatic stress disorder" (PTSD; American Psychiatric Association, 1980). *The Longman Dictionary of Psychology and Psychiatry* gives the following definition for PTSD:

> An anxiety disorder produced by an uncommon, extremely stressful event (e.g., assault, rape, military combat, flood, earthquake, death camp, torture, car accident, head trauma), and characterized by (a) reexperiencing the trauma in painful recollections or recurrent dreams or nightmares, (b) diminished responsiveness (emotional anesthesia or numbing), with disinterest in significant activities and with feelings of detachment and estrangement from others, and (c) such symptoms as exaggerated startle response, disturbed sleep, difficulty in concentrating or remembering, guilt about surviving when others did not, and

avoidance of activities that call the traumatic event to mind. (Goldenson, 1984, p. 573)

As a family stress researcher and therapist, I have seen the same disorder affect whole family systems. A victimizing event may have happened to one or both parents when they were children; they teach their children to numb their emotions, to stay disconnected from other people, to distrust others. Unless those family rules are changed, when those children grow up and become parents, they will also pass the disorder on to the next generation. In this way, post traumatic stress disorder can be found in families as well as individuals.

There are commonalities, therefore, between individual victimization and family victimization. The theory of victimization explains what happens to both: They suffer (a) feelings of helplessness, (b) shattered assumptions of fairness and order, and (c) shame and loss of self-esteem.

SELF-BLAME: IS IT HELPFUL?

Self-blame by the victim may be adaptive at times, but *only* when the blame is directed to *behavior*; it is not adaptive if it is directed to one's character. According to Ronnie Janoff-Bulman (1985), a psychologist, it may be functional for a victimized person to say, "I did a stupid thing, but I am *not* a stupid person" (p. 29). Likewise, it is functional for a victimized family to say collectively, "We did something wrong, but we are *not* a bad family." However, if a victimized family perceives the bad event or situation as happening to them because they are losers, tainted, or marked, they will have a harder time overcoming the victimization (and will stay in crisis longer) than if they feel that they as a family have the capability to change their behaviors and rules for interacting.

Family treatment centers for drug and alcohol addiction operate on the assumption that *family system behaviors and rules can and do change*, thus releasing the family from its maladaptive state. The families of incest and perpetrators of violence also can learn new behaviors; they must accept the principle that their adaptation to the abuse is dysfunctional but they themselves are not diseased or "bad." Frequent adaptive or defense mechanisms, such as denial, isolation, or inexpressiveness, and keeping secrets, are all dysfunctional for families as a whole.

A cognitive recovery is needed. The family must recognize and accept what was under its control, what was not, what won't ever be, and why. Danieli (1985) explains:

> Having been helpless does not mean that one is a helpless person; having witnessed or experienced evil does not mean that the world as a whole is evil; having been betrayed does not mean that betrayal is an overriding human behavior; having been victimized does not necessarily mean that one has to live one's life in constant readiness for its reenactment; having been treated as dispensable does not mean that one is worthless; and, taking the painful risk of bearing witness does not mean that the world will listen, learn, change, or become a better place. (p. 308)

CHRONIC THREAT OF VICTIMIZATION FROM OUTSIDE THE FAMILY

For some families, victimization may not be a present reality but, instead, is a constant *threat*. They would include families living where terrorism is highly possible, families of high military officials who would bring high ransoms, families who must because of poverty live where the danger of rape and murder are ever present. Other families live in constant fear of the possibility of nuclear explosion, either from nearby generators (as in Chernobyl and Three Mile Island) or from military missiles (set off either intentionally or by error). Yet other families are chronically victimized when they must, because of discrimination and prejudice, live in communities that shun and shame them.

All these situations constitute a constant threat of victimization, but since the families do not know *if or when* the overpowering event will happen, the element of ambiguity makes the potential of helplessness even more salient. Without certainty and facts, families are less able to take the necessary precautions to protect themselves from harm. Obviously, choices are not always possible for families. They do not always have the economic resources and opportunity to move, or to live in safer places. Their stress levels go up or they get dangerously passive. Both are a problem for such families.

CHRONIC VICTIMIZATION FROM INSIDE THE FAMILY

The threats of victimization I have just discussed come primarily from outside the family: politics, discrimination, macroeconomics, and natural disasters. Chronic threat of victimization also can come from *inside* the family, and then the negative effects are likely to be even greater. For a family to live under the constant threat of violence, incest, or drunkenness is a form of terrorism that often only the family knows about. There is a terrorist at work inside the family who overpowers (physically or psychologically) and erodes the self-esteem of family members, produces feelings of helplessness and inadequacy in them, and shatters their assumptions of fairness in the world. So victimized, family members are immobilized and cannot move out of danger. They begin to feel they deserve the bad treatment.

Nevertheless, some families who have lived in constant danger seem to be invincible. They survive everything. Others, however, become too precautionary in their way of living and overprotect the children, not allowing them to explore the outside world. They teach their children suspicion, distrust, and the inevitability of pain. We see this theme clinically in families that always see the negative side even in positive situations. This theme, by the way, is also present in many Woody Allen films (see especially *Annie Hall, Manhattan*, and *Hannah and Her Sisters*). Pessimism, distrust, and pain are the rule in some families; optimism, trust, and joy are the rule in others.

Reality lies somewhere in the middle. For most people, their family world was, for the most part, a good and fair place in which to live, but for many others there was injustice. Family scholars and professionals need to recognize that a dark side of family life exists alongside the positive, romanticized side. Families can be victimizing instead of protecting. If they do not recognize this problem, they cannot begin to change it.

Values and Belief Systems

In family stress theory, values and belief systems are predicted to play a major role in determining how a family responds to a chronic and stressful situation (see Boss, 1987). If the family values mastery over fatalism, action over passivity, or control over acceptance for "the way things are," those beliefs will make a difference in how a catastrophic event is perceived and responded to. From my observations, families with resources are more mastery oriented and rely more heavily on active behaviors and technology to overcome problems; they also rely more heavily on self-help information than on peer support groups where feelings are shared; that is, their major strategy is to seek out information to solve problems and reduce stress. In sum, the rich more than the poor and males more than females seem to be mastery oriented and active in their response to victimization from an over-powering and traumatic event.

We do not know, however, whether a passive and fatalistic orientation *precedes* or *follows* poverty, poor families having fewer resources and, therefore, less power. A passive, fatalistic belief system may result from situations in which families have no resources and are powerless. Being victimized is a situation of powerlessness for the family. Ascertaining a family's belief system will, I believe, be a necessary first step in determining, first, how the victimizing event is perceived and, second, how helplessness and humiliation can be overcome in their recovery. The answers will determine what kind of support system or information system such families will accept to recover from their crisis.

CULTURAL VIOLENCE AND VICTIMIZATION

We hear about the mugging of elderly women who simply are walking home with groceries. Violence has become a part of American culture. In psychological research conducted at several colleges in the United States and Canada, 35% of the men who participated voluntarily indicated some likelihood of committing a rape if there was no chance that they would be caught (Russell, 1982). In a study of 254 police officers from two urban and two rural southeastern communities, 78% believe that women provoke rape by their appearance or behavior (Field & Bienen, 1980). Bad things can happen to good people in a culture where violence is accepted.

Do you remember grade school? There was always a bully. At least one. Dr. Dan Olwens, a Swedish psychologist, found in a study that 20% of the school boys in his research population were involved in serious bullying and victimization. Dr. Nathaniel Floyd in Westchester, New York, is using this research to develop programs to teach grade school students how to manage bullying. He says that a school bully is usually a victim at home; that an abusive family system is the strongest contributing factor to bullying on the playground. The bully is really trying to make the victim protect him- or herself because bullies themselves feel threatened when vulnerable kids remind them of their humiliation and lack of power. So the bully constantly teases, desperately trying to get a victim who will say, "No, stop that! I won't let you treat me that way." According to the Swedish research, placating doesn't help; the most effective strategy is to oppose the bully and to take a more active rather than a passive stance (Hildebrand, 1987).

I propose here that victimization starts at home with child abuse; then the child is sent out to the playground where there is a bully or two there to hurt the child some more or to teach how to hurt others. Then in high school, "bully instincts" are in demand and highly rewarded in contact sports (e.g., hockey or football). In college, fraternities may still haze new members in a sophisticated form of torture, which continues the training for victimizing (actual deaths have resulted). As time moves on, the early victims become increasingly serious about victimization: blaming, ridiculing, shaming, physically abusing people, creating scape-goats in the workplace, homicide, mass murders, and, if they have children, starting the cycle all over again. They may then end up bullying or victimizing their aged and now weakened parents. The cycle repeats and repeats.

That cycle of victimization is not congruent if we are to have a humane society. In truth, we are a blaming society. Theoretically, blaming is linked to victimization. Let me give you some examples of just how blaming we are as a society.

Small family farmers in America are in trouble today. Some farmers are poor managers, it is true, and some have done a bad job and deserve to go bankrupt. But for the most part, there are many farmers who have done a good job but still are losing the farm. It is not their fault, yet they are being blamed. They are being blamed not only by the banks but by the older generation. Elderly parents—their own and their neighbors'—criticize them: "We survived the depression, why can't you survive this?" Thus the hardworking people who are losing family farms through no personal fault are shamed.

The older, critical generation never knew about 18% interest rates. They never experienced bankers who encouraged the overextension of loans. They never knew about a modern technology that now makes small farms obsolete. They just blame the victims. When a family is in trouble and failing, the community often withdraws from them. We tend to pull away from losers because in our competitive society we value winning. There are still people who blame rape victims ("she shouldn't have been there"); there are still people who blame children who are sexually abused ("they are seductive").

A Blaming Society for Vietnam Vets and Their Families

On Memorial Day weekend, 1986, a woman went to a graduation at the University of Chicago. It took place within a day or two of the Vietnam vets' Memorial Day parade. Although it was 13 years late, Chicago finally held a parade for its Vietnam vets. This woman had opposed the Vietnam War and had campaigned for Eugene McCarthy in 1968. She had been horrified by the Chicago riots during the Democratic party's convention. She intended not to have anything to do with the men and women who had participated in that war. After watching the parade, however, she wrote:

> The recent Memorial Day parade in Chicago honoring finally the homecoming of the men and women from the war in Viet Nam was a surprise. They were now aging veterans, but it was better late than never to honor them. It was such a bad war that we blamed the soldiers who were fighting it while we stood by in righteous protest. (Lawrence, 1986)

Many of us did that. We all thought we were doing the right thing but, instead of negating the idea of the war, we hurt a lot of young men and women who were in Vietnam and should not have been blamed for the war itself. They were already victims; we doubled their victimization by blaming them for the catastrophe.

THE THEORY OF A JUST WORLD

Where does all this judging and blaming come from? I believe it stems from the just world theory (see Chapter 6). If you believe in a just world, then, logically, nothing bad can happen to good families. When something bad happens to someone we know, somehow we have to isolate that person. Were a defective child born into our family or a family member to come down with a terminal illness, we would automatically have to perform a shift in our heads to accept rather than blame our family member. I talked with one man who had been missing in action in Vietnam for years; he told me how terrible being a POW had been at first. He felt that it was his fault because he believed in a just world. According to his perception of why he was taken prisoner, he had not run fast enough to catch the helicopter that picked up his buddy, and he blamed himself for his capture. Subsequently, however, he changed his perception. I asked him when this had happened. He said it was after he came back and studied the politics of the war. Whom did he blame now, I asked, and he said, "Congress." He moved the blame outside of himself. He said he finally stopped blaming himself for a situation that was not under his control.

Those of us who believe in a just world theory have trouble tolerating the illogical or believing that something bad can happen to good people;

or, the opposite, that something good can happen to bad people. The basis of this just world theory is the assumption of mastery—that we are in control of our own destiny—as a primary value orientation. This is a very American idea, and it has gotten us into trouble at times. It also may be why we are such a violent society.

FLAWS IN THE JUST WORLD THEORY

The Myth of Equal Power

The two basic flaws at the heart of the just world theory are discussed in this and the following subsection. First of all, the value of mastery and being in control of one's own destiny is predicated on the belief that everyone has equal power and that we all have knowledge, skills, and resources to control our own destiny. This is an unrealistic belief because, for example, frail elderly people, babies, children, and unemployed people without skills do not have the resources that allow taking charge of one's own destiny. It is true for all of us when we are in a weakened condition. We cannot make decisions when we have no choices; we cannot manage if there are no resources to distribute.

The Assumption That Only Incompetent People Are Helpless

Competent people, even those with resources, can become helpless. Victimization does not happen only to the weak and frail; it can happen to the best of us. Brainwashing and torture can change a mastery-oriented person within a short time. If the trauma is powerful enough, even competent people can become victims. They are taught to become helpless through reinforcement.

Learned helplessness is a concept that was first described empirically by people who were studying animal learning (Overmier & Seligman, 1967; Peterson & Seligman, 1983). They set up some experiments in which dogs were put in a cage and exposed to unavoidable and inescapable electric shocks. The dogs ran around in the cages trying to avoid the shock and, within 24 hours, they showed the symptoms of helplessness. In the initial experiments, the researchers made avoidance possible and the dog felt relief, but then they arranged the electric shocks so the dog could not avoid them. Giving first positive and then negative reinforcement is called intermittent reinforcement; it confuses the subject. Three things happened to the dogs in these experiments. Anyone who has ever worked with victims knows the same thing can happen to human beings.

First, there was a *motivational deficit*. The dogs no longer tried to get away from the shock; they just lay down. Such passivity in the face of danger happens to men and women as well, especially when the situation seems illogical and escape, hopeless.

Second, a *cognitive deficit* set in; although there was a way to avoid the shock, the dogs failed to learn it because of the confusing reinforcement. So they just gave up. When a person has been wounded enough, he or she will just lie down and take it, even if escape is possible. Men who have been in prison camps and battered women have told me me this.

Third, *emotional deficit* was experienced. The dogs showed no reactions. I have seen this same lack of affect in clients who have been victimized. One woman reported to me with equally flat affect both the horrifying and good events in her life: "Yeah, my boyfriend burned me all over with cigarettes" "Yes, I found a job." She had learned to seal off her emotions in order to survive the horror of victimization.

When catastrophe happens to people, such as in the Holocaust, child abuse, battering of women, or brutality during war or imprisonment, victims often hide their emotion. Hence we do not see their pain. We may blame the victim when, for example, a woman goes right back to her violent husband and, unquestionably, for another beating. She is like the dogs who lay down on the bottom of the cage and just let the electric shocks happen again and again. It could happen to any of us under conditions of intermittent reinforcement.

Learned Helplessness in Families

Let me tell you about family situations in which the same thing happens. Because of intermittent reinforcement, binge drinking is harder for a family to deal with than daily tippling. When a family member is drunk every day, the behavior is predictable. But if he or she drinks only once in a while and the family never quite knows when, then it is harder for them to manage the problem because of its uncertainty. If a parent beats a child regularly and is always mean, it is clear that he or she is the enemy; but if that parent is affectionate one minute and strikes the next, that is intermittent reinforcement. It produces helplessness and further victimization.

Families of the missing-in-action have had that sort of ambiguity: now you see them, now you don't; it's in the news—yes, they're alive, no, they aren't. The Iranian hostage families also suffered the effects of such intermittent reinforcement.

EMPOWERING VICTIMIZED FAMILIES

At the crux of the family's feelings of helplessness is ambiguity caused by intermittent reinforcement. When a family is helpless, it cannot function, and so, family victimization is classified as a crisis (see Figure 4.3). The hopeful side of victimization is this: If helplessness can be learned, it can also be unlearned. The theory tells us that empowerment will come from (a) regaining self-esteem in family members and pride in the family as a team, (b) regaining control over what happens to the family members, individually and as a group, (c) making some bit of sense out of what happened by finding some meaning in what happened, and (d) sharing with others while actively working to prevent it from happening again.[4]

There are, however, blocks to the empowerment process. The first is the inequality of races; the second is the inequality of genders. Racial minority families have fewer resources and opportunities for shaping their own destinies. And in almost all cultures and subcultures, females are still socialized to be more passive and submissive than are males. They are more likely to be victimized if passivity is perceived as their role. Infanticide and bride burning are extreme examples, but they still take place in some cultures. The feminization of poverty is a less extreme but more prevalent example of gender inequality in America. Empowerment is difficult, if not impossible, in such settings.

POINTS TO REMEMBER

(1) Families as well as individuals can be victimized.

(2) Victimization is defined as the overpowering of a person or family with physical or psychological trauma that results in feelings of helplessness, distrust of the world, and humiliation.

(3) Family victimization is an example of crisis since the traumatized family is immobilized and in danger.

(4) The source of victimization can be both inside and outside the family.

(5) Recovery from victimization is called empowerment.

(6) Behaviors produced by victimization are passivity, isolation, feelings of helplessness, and distrust of the world. Behaviors of recovery (empowerment) are finding and developing options, making

choices, getting information, finding peer support groups, and developing future plans.

(7) Empowerment cannot be achieved when there is a power differential between genders and among families.

NOTES

1. Portions of this chapter are based on the author's presidential address, "Victimization Inside and Outside the Family: Prevention and Recovery," presented at the annual meeting of the Groves Conference on Marriage and the Family, London, England, July 16-20, 1986.

2. From an interview broadcast on NBC Network News, Monday, March 10, 1986.

3. This same premise was raised in 1980 when the Iranians took 53 Americans hostage at the American Embassy in Teheran. A task force on families and catastrophe was organized by Charles Figley at Purdue University. Earlier research findings, derived primarily from data involving victimization and recovery for the MIA families collected by the Center for Prisoner of War Studies in San Diego, were used to develop recommendations that were presented to the State Department. The task force urged the State Department to (a) arrange a debriefing period with the hostages before reintegrating them with their families, (b) to support family meetings and telephone communications, and (c) to respect family privacy and support during the absence of and after reunion with the hostages. The major point of the report was that families of victims also are victimized and, therefore, must also be supported.

4. Nancy Spungen was found stabbed to death in a Manhattan hotel room in 1978, apparently by her lover, punk rock star Sid Vicious. The story of Sid Vicious and Nancy Spungen is a story of victimization. The mother of Nancy, Deborah Spungen, thought at first the only way to end her own pain was to kill herself. Instead, she transformed her grief into activity, helping other parents of murder victims by opening a victims' advocacy center and by studying social policy law so that she can help to shape legislation and lobby for families of murder victims ("Sid and Nancy," 1987).

FURTHER READING

Blank, A. S. Jr. (1982). Stresses of war: The example of Viet Nam. In L. Goldberger & S. Breznitz (Eds.), *Handbook of stress*. New York: Free Press.

Boss, P. (1986, July). *Victimization*. Presidential address presented at the Groves Conference on Marriage and the Family, London, England.

Festinger, L. (1957). *A theory of cognitive dissonance*. Stanford, CA: Stanford University Press.

Figley, C. (Ed.). (1978). *Stress disorders among Vietnam veterans*. New York: Brunner/Mazel.

Figley, C. (Ed.). (1985). *Trauma and its wake*. New York: Brunner/Mazel.

Fossum, M. A., & Mason, M. J. (1986). *Facing shame*. New York: W. W. Norton.

Hunter, E. J. (1983). Treating the military captive family. In F. Kaslow & R. Ridenour (Eds.), *The military family: Dynamics and treatment*. New York: Guilford Press.

Janoff-Bulman, R., & Frieze, I. H. (1983). Reactions to victimization [Special issue]. *Journal of Social Issues, 39*(2).

Kastrup, M., Lunde, I., Ortmann, J., & Kemp Genefke, I. (1986, July). *Families of torture: Consequences and possibilities for rehabilitation.* Paper presented at Groves Conference on Marriage and the Family, London, England.

Lerner, M. J. (1971). Justice, guilt, and veridical perception. *Journal of Personality and Social Psychology, 20,* 127-135.

Lerner, M. J., & Simmons, C. (1966). Observers' reaction to the innocent victim: Compassion or rejection? *Journal of Personality and Social Psychology, 4,* 203-210.

Phillemer, K. A., & Wolf, R. S. (Eds.). (1986). *Elder abuse.* Dover, MA: Auburn House.

Sontag, S. (1979). *Illness as a metaphor.* New York: Vintage Books.

CHAPTER

9

Where Did We Come From and Where Are We Now?

LOOKING BACK

I first met Reuben Hill when he was assigned by the military to consult on my research on missing-in-action families. We had stimulating discussions—and a few arguments. He became my strongest supporter. I think of him as my intellectual mentor in family stress theory.

The work in this book springs from his work. He fully intended to give me his reactions to each chapter as I wrote. But life does not always go as we plan. Reuben Hill died in Norway on September 21, 1985.

I met often with Reuben in his office at the University of Minnesota to discuss ideas about family stress. But the last time we met, we did not discuss the book. Instead, he asked for some help. He was on his way to Oslo, Norway, where he was to teach a course on family theory to clinicians. We talked for more than two hours about linkages between family theory and the practice of family therapy, a connection that is critical for understanding family stress. Then we spent another hour talking about feminist theory as it relates to family stress.

When Reuben Hill left that afternoon, his arms were loaded with things he wanted to read. He had asked to borrow some books and papers on family therapy and on feminist theory.[1]

I can still see him smiling as he walked away from McNeal Hall, arms loaded with books. Although retired, he was still a hardworking professor, starting on a new quest to Norway, still learning and still developing theory.

I tell you this story because it was Reuben Hill who was the first to conceptualize family stress theory (see Hill, 1949/1971). He is still known worldwide as "the father of family stress theory." The contents of this book are a further conceptualization and development of his original work on the ABC-X model of family stress and the roller-coaster model of family crisis. Perhaps he would not have agreed with my reconceptualizations, but I do know that we would have had some good discussions, and perhaps some more arguments. What we did agree on always was that if family theory was to move forward, researchers and therapists must talk together and link their ideas.

The Legacy of Reuben Hill and Others

In the Talmud and the Bible, we see that families have been concerned with events of change, trouble, disaster, and ambiguity since the beginning of recorded time. The systematic study of these phenomena by scholars, however, is relatively recent. Family stress research began at the University of Michigan and the University of Chicago during the upheavals of the depression of the 1930s. Economic loss was the stressor event in the first studies by Angell (1936/1965) and Cavan and Ranck (1938). These sociologists used the case study approach; that is, they applied social-psychological theory to examinations of families as well as of the individuals in the family. The family was viewed as an "organization that is in the constant process of adaptation to changing conditions" (Angell, 1936/1965, p. 14). Not unlike some present-day researchers such as David Reiss (1981), who wrote about the family's change process, Angell saw families as entering "a new phase of this tentative process" (1936/1965, p. 14).

Based on his research, Angell derived the two major determinants of a family's reaction to sudden loss of income: (a) *integration*, which he defined as the family's common interest, affection, sense of economic interdependence, and other bonds of coherence and unity, and (b) *adaptability*, which he defined as the flexibility of the family unit in discussion and decision making. These early findings remain unchallenged today; current researchers present similar findings regarding family strengths (Olson et al., 1983; Stinnett & DeFrain, 1986). But already in 1936, Angell found that the most important characteristic of strong families was flexibility, since "plastic" families (those in which roles were interchangeable rather than rigid) were best equipped to surmount trouble. He concluded that "even a moderate degree of *adaptability* will pull families with any *integration* at all through all but the worst crises" (p. 181). In other words, family flexibility is even more critical than family coherence when there is high stress.

In 1938, Cavan and Ranck added to this work with a longitudinal study of families before and during the Depression, spanning the years 1927 to 1935. Supporting the findings of Angell, the two investigators found that a family's previous methods of meeting difficulties were related to how they met a current difficulty; that is, functional families, even when Depression losses were great, continued to be functional, whereas previously dysfunctional families became more dysfunctional.

Unemployment continued to be the major focus of family stress investigations even beyond the Depression (e.g., both Komarovsky, 1940, and Cavan, 1959, studied unemployed males). Then in 1946, a Columbia University researcher named Koos, focused on economic stress from a different perspective. For the first time, this researcher made explicit the high stress of urban living by studying *family ability to solve troubles and crisis* in a New York City slum. His major contribution to the literature was his "profile of trouble" (1946, p. 107) upon which Reuben Hill (1949) then based "the roller-coaster pattern of response to stress." Koos made an early plea for social supports to aid families in managing with high stress:

> A first need, if the effect of trouble is to be minimized, is the reconstruction of the family as a family. This is *not* to be construed as saying that it is up to the family. Quite the opposite. As our industrial culture has provided the elements leading to family disintegration, so must that culture now provide (through social organization) for the reconstitution of the family. (p. 123)

In his 1949 study of families stressed with father absence during World War II, Reuben Hill made a major contribution to theory by focusing on the family as a culturally conditioned organization reflecting the state of the culture and, at the same time, internal familial behaviors. Based on the earlier findings of Angell (1936/1965), Cavan and Ranck (1938), Komarovsky (1940), and Koos (1946), Hill developed a list of 10 items to test family adequacy in relation to the twin concepts of family *integration* (coherence) and *adaptability* (flexibility). He labeled these 10 items "family resources": (a) previous success in meeting family crisis; (b) nonmaterialistic goals predominate; (c) flexibility and willingness to shift traditional roles of husband and wife or father and mother, if necessary; (d) acceptance of responsibility by all family members in performing family duties; (e) willingness to sacrifice personal interest to attain family objectives; (f) pride in the family tree and ancestral traditions; (g) presence of strong patterns of emotional interdependence and unity; (h) high participation as a family in joint activities; (i) presence of egalitarian patterns of family control and decision making; and (j) strong affectional ties between father-mother, father-children, mother-children, children-children (Hill, 1949, pp. 17-18). These resources were were found to mediate the stress of family separation and reunion brought about by World War II. Of the many contributions to the literature stemming from this study, the most lasting has been the ABC-X model (Hill, 1949, 1958) and the roller-coaster model of family crisis (Hill, 1949). (These were defined briefly in Chapter 2; see Figure 2.4.)

The Roller-Coaster Model of Family Crisis

The roller-coaster model of family adjustment after crisis developed by Reuben Hill in 1949; and adapted by others (Boss, 1986; Hansen & Hill, 1964) illustrates familial adjustment to *crisis*. According to the model, the family may go into crisis after the onset of a stressor event. Crisis, of course, is the *period of disorganization* in which previous interactions and behaviors for managing and solving problems become inadequate, inoperable, or blocked. Then, with the time depending on the ability to change, the family reaches a turning point, begins to reorganize, and goes into what Hill (1949) called the *period of recovery*. Finally, the family reaches a new *level of reorganization* above, below, or equal to the one experienced before the onset of the stressor event. (See Figure 2.6.)

What this means is that a family does not have to be destroyed by a crisis. It can recover, although its level of functioning may be different from what it was at the time the event occurred. This point needs further empirical verification, but it is supported by clinical observations. Koos's and Hill's premises of variation in levels of recovery for families that have been in crisis are seen again and again in family therapy.

Family crisis has been defined in this book as a disturbance in system equilibrium so acute and so strong that the family is at least temporarily immobilized and stuck. It cannot function. Because of that immobilization, there may even be threat of injury or death. This definition is generally congruent with the definition developed by Reuben Hill in his original ABC-X model. In this book, however, I make a sharp distinction between crisis and stress. That is a necessary conceptual clarification in family stress theory.

The ABC-X Model of Family Stress

In 1958, Hill's ABC-X model provided a bridge between the work of family sociologists and that of social workers who dealt with multi-problem families. His stress model (A, the provoking event or stressor; B, the resources or strengths the family has at the time of the event; and C, the meaning that the family, individually and collectively, attaches to the event) became the foundation of family stress theory and has been heuristically presented in this book and elsewhere (Boss, 1987). Hill's ABC-X model is, however, more an important reference point than a testable model. Its value lies primarily in providing exploratory direction to investigations about family stress and crisis. Too often, however, scholars have mixed up stress and crisis in using the ABC-X model. Note the distinction between stress and crisis as I adapted Hill's model in Figure 4.2.

**Linking the ABC-X Model
to the Roller-Coaster Model**

. I have emphasized the difference between Reuben Hill's ABC-X model of family *stress* and his roller-coaster model of family *crisis*. Nevertheless, the two are linked. The roller-coaster model (as I adapted it) illustrates the *breaking point* at which crisis occurs (see Figure 2.6). Day-to-day fluctuations of stress are depicted as increasingly wild gyrations until, finally, the family structure breaks under the strain (like an overloaded bridge) and is no longer functional. I believe this crisis model represents a magnification of only one portion of the broken X factor. Figure 2.4 shows crisis as a state separate from high stress (note the broken line). Crisis is something other than simply the highest point of the stress continuum. Crisis therefore is not a continuous variable. It is a categorical variable. You are either immobilized or you are not.

My adaptation of the ABC-X model in this book illustrates the process by which a family avoids the breaking point or reaches it. It is a conceptualization of the process of family stress *management* that helps us to understand strong families as well as those in trouble, and therefore to understand family strengths as well as weaknesses. Because the ABC-X model is essentially a model of prevention, it does not focus on recovery from crisis. It presents stress as a normal part of everyday family life, not just as disaster. The model does not focus on recovery.

It is the roller-coaster model that helps us to understand family recovery because it pictures the disorganization and reorganization process in families. They are immobilized, hit bottom, and, we hope, turn around to begin the process of recovery. Although this model focuses on disaster, it allows for positive outcomes, since levels of recovery can be even higher than before the family fell into crisis.

WHERE WE ARE NOW AND WHERE WE NEED TO GO

My task in this book has been to present a conceptualization of family stress management to help you to better understand families, your own or those with which you work. My intention was not to offer answers on how to fix families. Given the diversity of American families, there is no one simple answer that is valid for all. A sound theoretical base, I believe, is a more useful starting point for finding answers to unique family stress situations.

Life is a struggle for some families but for many, life is boring if it lacks some degree of stress and challenge. Perception—not the professional's but the family's—is the key to understanding stressed families. Hence my focus on the *meaning* a family gives to an event or situation.

One example of the importance of family perception in predicting the outcome of stress is family boundary ambiguity: not knowing who is in and who is out of the family. I have presented this new variable, which is becoming part of family stress theory, to demonstrate that *a perceptual variable* can be conceptualized, measured, and documented as a predictor of families that can manage an event of loss as well as families that do not (see Blackburn, Greenberg, & Boss, 1988; Boss, 1977, 1980a, 1987; Boss & Greenberg, 1984; Boss, Pearce-McCall, & Greenberg, 1988). Although substantial empirical testing continues, the variable of boundary ambiguity is demonstrating its general theoretical strength as an approach to understanding how a family sees the loss of a member. The focus, therefore, is less on the event and more on the *meaning* the event has for that family. What one family sees as hopeless another may see as a challenge; although one family may see an ill member as already gone, another family may act as if nothing is wrong at all. The variable of boundary ambiguity is one example of a barrier to stress management in families with long-term stress.

Denial is another new variable in the family stress literature. Therapists have long known of the power of denial in families when a terminal illness is diagnosed or addiction is a problem. Finally, a family's values and beliefs are also critical to the management of family stress.

These three concepts (boundary ambiguity, denial, and values and beliefs) make up the internal context of family stress. Certainly there are others, but these are examples of the dimensions the family is able to change and control, depending on their perceptions of what is happening to them.

The internal context of family stress, however, cannot be understood without also looking at it in relation to the external context—those dimensions the family cannot control. I have argued elsewhere that the family's belief in fatalism may be related more to economics than to culture. Families need resources to manage stress. When families are poor and discriminated against, their resources to solve problems are not equal to those of families who have higher incomes and are not identified solely as members of minority groups. Even individuals within families have unequal resources; women in all cultures, including our own, still have fewer economic resources than do men. We cannot expect families to solve problems if they have no options or if their resources to manage stress are meager. So, too, we cannot expect individuals in families to manage stress well if they have few resources and no choices. One cannot exercise management without resources; one cannot make decisions without choices. It is true that in some families, the lack of resources and choices may be more perceptual than real, but when low-income children, women, and minority families are genuinely deprived, it is *more* than perception.

Problem-solving behaviors and management styles, therefore, have strong links to gender and ethnicity more because of economics than because of ineptness. If a battered wife goes back home where she will be hurt again, we must be cautious about blaming the victim. Until she has someplace else to go and safety for her children, she may have no other choice. When we look at families who live in urban slums or in dying rural areas, we must be cautious about blaming them for their situations. Their lack of options may stem from larger political and economic issues that are not always under the family's control.

Context matters, therefore, in the study of family stress management. What happens outside the family's control—the cultural, historic, developmental, constitutional, and economic dimensions—is critical to understanding how a family *perceives* and then reacts to a particular event or situation. Having a family member in the military forces was perceived and reacted to very differently during World War II than during the Vietnam War. When a nation is divided over participation in a war, the perceptions of individuals even within families are also divided and stress will be higher for all. Families of World War II soldiers, for example, reacted very differently to the war's end than did families of military men and women who had been in Vietman. In order to understand these familial perceptions and responses, consequently, the external context had to be understood. We have only recently begun to consider this larger picture of family stress for the Vietnam veterans.

CHANGE IN STRESSED FAMILIES

Families that suffer from too much stress have essentially two choices: (a) to lower the stress on their systems or (b) to increase their supports and resources. Both options require change.

Most families move in the necessary directions for change without professional help. They are flexible, and yet there is team work. Family members talk to friends, attend peer support groups, talk to pastors or family doctors, read books, or take up some new activity, such as going back to school and taking classes in a field that is new to them. (As stated earlier, there are gender differences in activities chosen that need to be investigated further.) Families that are able to take such actions often manage their stress and therapists never see them.

On the other hand, some families are stressed and therapists don't see them, either, since therapy is often limited to those with economic resources. Low-income families are much less able to seek professional help unless *crisis* brings them to the attention of public authorities and attention becomes required. We know little therefore about the many poor families who manage stress competently and heroically. More research is needed on the competent poor families who find ways to manage stress on their own.

And finally, some families change without experiencing crises (at least, as far as the outside observer can see). They show up frequently in research studies where they are classed as invulnerable, strong, or healthy families. They are adaptable (flexible) and draw close together as a team in their responses to the inevitable pressures of everyday family life.

But adaptability (flexibility) and cohesion (togetherness) may not always be good for families. Context may determine whether adaptation and cohesion are functional or dysfunctional. It may be that when the stressor event is introduced to a family by something *externally*, adaptability and cohesion are what make it possible for stress to be managed. But when a stressor event is introduced by something or someone *internally*, the family may need to *change* rather than adapt and *gain distance* rather than draw closer together in order to manage stress. This contextual view, I believe, provides a richer base for further study of stressed families.

CHANGE IN STRAINED FAMILIES

Unfortunately, not all families are invulnerable. When the level of stress increases, such a family shows signs of strain and the possibilities of crisis.[2] Unable to manage their own stress level, the family reaches out for professional help. Such families respond well to educational information on stress management as well as to psychotherapy. The latter may provide necessary insights and supports to change family rules, to push for individuation from a family-of-origin, and to push for tolerance of both separateness and closeness in the family system; nevertheless, these families also need information on the complexity of the event that is stressing them. This blend of information and therapy is called the *psychoeducational approach*. Families join peer groups, attend lectures, read, and gather information about their particular situation as well as participate in family therapy. Thus far, this psychoeducational approach has been found to be very effective in working with at least two types of difficult and highly stressed family systems: schizophrenic and alcoholic (Gurman & Kniskern, 1986).

CHANGE IN FAMILIES IN CRISIS

Stressed families that are not flexible or open to change are most likely to fall into crisis. They exemplify what Carl Whitaker (personal communication, 1973), a pioneer in family therapy, meant when he said, "Some families have to get worse before they can get better." The psychoeducational approach may not be sufficient for these families. The primary therapeutic goal here is to break the family's denial system; for this, group work has been most effective. Alcoholics Anonymous and Parents Anonymous have, for example, been most successful in achieving this goal. Indeed, such groups have been more successful than individual psychotherapy with families (or family members) in which denial is the major block to change in interaction.

Nevertheless, in families in which abuse, incest, or threat to life exists, a straightforward and immediate confrontation is necessary from the family professional: educator or therapist. Many states have laws mandating the immediate report of such conditions to appropriate authorities. Having an abusive parent arrested or a neglected child removed from the home no doubt will precipitate a full-blown family crisis, but that cannot be any worse than the hidden victimization that existed in the family before.

THE DILEMMA REMAINS: DO WE FOCUS ON THE INDIVIDUAL OR THE FAMILY?

It is indeed possible for one member of a family to be immobilized (in crisis) and for the system to continue to function. The family as a unit can deny what is happening and look fine to the outsider; everyone works hard to cover up for the person in trouble.

According to my earlier definition of crisis, then, such a family, *as a whole*, is not in crisis, but it is strained and in trouble. A cover-up cannot go on very long without reaching a breaking point—a crisis. It is often convenient for such families to say that if it were not for Junior (or whoever the scapegoat is), this family would be just fine. The overall strain (and possible victimization) in the system is denied and the stress is dumped exclusively on the family scapegoat.

Scapegoating raises an ethical issue. Suppose one person in the family is in crisis—say suicidal or dangerously ill—but the rest of the family goes about its work as if nothing were wrong. If this situation is not a crisis in the eyes of the family *as a whole*, it is a crisis (immobilization) in the eyes of that one family member. The ethical issue for the family professional is whose interests are to be served: the individual's or the family's?

As far as I am concerned, the answer is clear. An individual's life takes precedence over loyalty to family unity. When we do not want to deal with individual victimization resulting from incest, addiction, violence, or neglect, then we are preserving the family at too high a cost. This is romanticizing the family. However much we may value the family, we cannot, at the same time, close our eyes to its darker side. The potential is there.

But family stress is another matter. It represents a lighter side of family life. It represents change; it is normal and natural, even fun at times, especially when it is invited. In a complex human system in which change and maturation are inevitable, in a society in which competition and mastery are valued, the welfare of families and the people in them may rest primarily on the ability to manage rather than to avoid stress. Toward this end, I have addressed this book.

POINTS TO REMEMBER

(1) Family life is a struggle for some families, but for others family life is boring without competition or challenge. Family stress, therefore, can be positive as well as negative.

(2) The level of family stress can be managed so that there are fewer crises across the life cycle, or so that, when they do occur, the family can recover as quickly as possible.

(3) A family can recover to an even higher level of functioning as a result of a crisis.

(4) It is not always good for a family to be resistant to crisis. A family that is too stoic and rigid can also cause stress for its members. It may be better sometimes for a family to let the stress level rise unchecked, even going into crisis, rather than pushing down "the family thermostat" and keeping the family peaceful at all costs.

(5) The variables of boundary ambiguity, denial, and belief systems are important in the explanation and prediction of family stress management. These variables are important for family professionals to understand as they plan for prevention and treatment.

(6) There are gender, racial, and cultural differences in how family stress is perceived and managed. More research is critically needed in this area.

(7) The ABC-X model is linked to the roller-coaster model up to the point of crisis. The roller-coaster model illustrates *crisis* and *recovery*, whereas the ABC-X model illustrates *stress management* and therefore *prevention* of crisis.

(8) Family adaptability (flexibility) is still the key to family stress management. It was found to be so in early family stress research and is still so today. However, today we also have empirical support for the importance of *perception* as the primary predictor of how or whether a family can manage their stress. There may be, therefore, some connection between how *flexible* a family is and how they *perceive* what is happening to them. The relationship between family adaptability and perception has not yet been established empirically, but family therapists often observe a correlation in recovering families. Further investigation is needed here.

(9) Stress is a continuous variable, whereas family crisis is a categorical variable. What this means is that a family can be in varying degrees of stress, but they are either in crisis or not. A family cannot be in a low degree of crisis. This difference between family stress and family

crisis is important to family professionals. Much more directive intervention is needed in times of crisis. Support and information may be more useful for managing stress.

(10) When stress is introduced to a family by something in the *external* context, the adaptability (flexibility) and integrity (cohesion) of the family are what make it possible for the stress to be managed. But when the stress is introduced by someone or something *internally*, the family may need to *change* rather than adapt and *establish some distance* rather than draw closer together. Research is needed to test these ideas about the contextual source of family stress.

NOTES

1. Reuben Hill took with him that day Goldner (1985), Hare-Musten (1978), Hoffman (1981), Thorne and Yalom (1982), and Weiner and Boss (1985).

2. David Reiss has said that only a family in crisis can change. My point is that healthy families may change without a crisis, but I agree that some families may need a crisis to bring about the malleability needed before change can occur.

FURTHER READING

Angell, R. C. (1965). *The family encounters the depression.* New York: Charles Scribner. (Original work published 1936)

Cavan, R. S. (1959). Unemployment: Crisis of the common man. *Marriage and Family Living, 21,* 139-146.

Cavan, R. S., & Ranck, K. H. (1938). *The family and the Depression.* Chicago: University of Chicago Press.

Gilligan, C. (1982). *In a different voice.* Cambridge: Harvard University Press.

Hansen, D., & Hill, R. (1964). Families under stress. In H. T. Christensen (Ed.), *Handbook of marriage and the family.* Chicago: Rand McNally.

Hansen, D., & Johnson, V. (1979). Rethinking family stress theory: Definitional aspects. In W. Burr, R. Hill, F. Nye, & I. Reiss (Eds.), *Contemporary theories about the family* (Vol. 1). New York: Free Press.

Hill, R. (1971). *Families under stress.* Westport, CT: Greenwood Press. (Original work published 1949)

Hill, R. (1958, February-March). Generic features of families under stress. *Social Casework, 49,* 139-150.

Hill, R. (1973). *Family life cycle: Critical role transitions.* Paper presented at the Thirteenth International Family Research Seminar, Paris.

Hill, R., & Hansen, D. A. (1962). Families in disaster. In G. W. Baker & E. W. Chapman (Eds.), *Man and society in disaster.* New York: Basic Books.

Komarovsky, M. (1940). *The unemployed man and his family.* New York: Dryden Press.

Koos, E. L. (1946). *Families in trouble.* New York: King's Crown Press.

Rapoport, L. (1965). The state of crisis: Some theoretical considerations. In H. Parad (Ed.), *Crisis intervention: Selected readings.* New York: Family Service Association of America.

Scherz, F. H. (1966). Family treatment concepts. *Social Casework, 47*(4), 234-240.

References

Adams, B. (1986). *The family: A sociological interpretation* (4th ed.). New York: Harcourt Brace Jovanovich.

Ahrons, C. R., & Rogers, R. H. (1987). *Divorced families.* New York: McGraw-Hill.

Akutagawa, R. (1952). *Rashomon and other stories* (T. Kojima, Trans.). Tokyo: Charles E. Tuttle.

Aldous, J. (1978). *Family careers: Developmental change in family.* New York: John Wiley.

American Psychiatric Association. (1980). *Diagnostic and statistical manual of mental disorders* (DSM III; 3rd ed.). Washington, DC: Author.

Angell, R. C. (1965). *The family encounters the Depression.* New York: Charles Scribner. (Original work published 1936)

Antonovsky, A. (1979). *Health, stress and coping.* San Francisco: Jossey- Bass.

Armstrong, L. (1979). *Kiss daddy goodnight.* New York: Simon & Schuster.

Arsenian, J., & Arsenian, J. M. (1948). Tough and easy cultures: A conceptual analysis. *Psychiatry, 11,* 377-385.

Bartlett, G. S., Houts, P. S., Byrnes, L. K., & Miller, R. W. (1983). The near disaster at Three Mile Island. In O. Hultaker & J. Trost (Eds.), *International Journal of Mass Emergencies and Disasters, 1*(1), 19-42.

Bernard, J. (1972). *The future of marriage.* New York: World Press.

Bettelheim, B. (1977). *The uses of enchantment: The meaning and importance of fairy tales.* New York: Random House.

Bianco, C. (1974). *The two rosetos.* Bloomington: Indiana University Press.

Biddle, B., & Thomas, E. (1966). *Role theory: Concepts and research.* New York: John Wiley.

Billings, A., & Moos, R. H. (1981). The role of coping responses and social resources in attenuating the stress of life events. *Journal of Behavioral Medicine, 10,* 57-189.

Black, C. (1981). *It will never happen to me.* Denver, CO: M.A.C. Printing and Publications.

Blackburn, J., Greenberg, J., & Boss, P. (1988). Coping with normative stress from loss and change: A longitudinal study of ranch and non-ranch widows. *Journal of Gerontological Social Work, 11*(2).

Bolin, R. C., & Bolton, P. A. (1983). Recovery in Nicaragua and the U.S A. In O. Hultaker & J. Trost (Eds.), *International Journal of Mass Emergencies and Disasters, 1*(1), 125-144.

Boss, P. G. (1975a). *Psychological father absence and presence: A theoretical formulation for an investigation into family systems interaction.* Unpublished doctoral dissertation, University of Wisconsin—Madison.

Boss, P. G. (1975b, November). Psychological father presence in the missing-in-action (MIA) family: Its effects on family functioning. *Proceedings: Third Annual Joint Medical Meeting Concerning POW/MIA Matters* (pp. 61-65). Center for Prisoner of War Studies, Naval Health Research Center, San Diego, CA.

Boss, P. G. (1977). A clarification of the concept of psychological father presence in families experiencing ambiguity of boundary. *Journal of Marriage and the Family, 39*(1), 141-151.

Boss, P. G. (1979). Theoretical influences on family policy. *Journal of Home Economics, 71*(3), 17-21.

Boss, P. G. (1980a). Normative family stress: Family boundary changes across the lifespan. *Family Relations, 29*(4), 445-450.

Boss, P. G. (1980b). The relationship of psychological father presence, wife's personal qualities, and wife/family dysfunction in families of missing fathers. *Journal of Marriage and the Family, 42*(3), 541-549.

Boss, P. G. (1980c). Précis prepared for the Emergency Meeting of the Task Force on Families of Catastrophe, February 4-5, 1980. In C. R. Figley (Ed.), *Mobilization: Part I. The Iranian crisis* (Final report of the Task Force on Families of Catastrophe). West Lafayette, IN: Purdue University Family Research Institute.

Boss, P. G. (1982, October). *The measurement of family boundary ambiguity: A general variable in family stress theory.* Paper presented at the National Council on Family Relations.

Boss, P. G. (1983a). Family separation and boundary ambiguity. In O. Hultaker & J. Trost (Eds.), *International Journal of Mass Emergencies and Disasters, 1*(1), 63-72.

Boss, P. G. (1983b). The marital relationship: Boundaries and ambiguities. In C. Figley & H. I. McCubbin (Eds.), *Stress and the family* (Vol. 2). New York: Brunner/Mazel.

Boss, P. G. (1986, July). *Victimization.* Presidential address presented to the Groves Conference on Marriage and the Family, London, England.

Boss, P. G. (1987). Family stress: Perception and context. In M. Sussman & S. Steinmetz (Eds.), *Handbook on marriage and the family* (pp. 695-723). New York: Plenum.

Boss, P. G., Caron, W., & Horbal, J. (1988). Alzheimer's disease and ambiguous loss. In C. Chilman, F. Cox, & E. Nunnally (Eds.), *Families in trouble.* Newbury Park, CA: Sage.

Boss, P. G., & Greenberg, J. (1984). Family boundary ambiguity: A new variable in family stress theory. *Family Process, 23*(4), 535-546.

Boss, P. G., McCubbin, H. I., & Lester, G. (1979). The corporate executive wife's coping patterns in response to routine husband-father absence. *Family Process, 18*(1), 79-86.

Boss, P. G., Pearce-McCall, D., & Greenberg, J. (1986). *The normative stress of adolescents leaving home in mid-life families* (U.S.D.A. NC-164 Regional Basebook Report). St. Paul: University of Minnesota Agricultural Experiment Station.

Boss, P. G., Pearce-McCall, D., & Greenberg, J. (1987). Normative loss in mid-life families: Rural, urban, and gender differences in rural families [Special issue]. *Family Relations.*

Boss, P. G., Pearce-McCall, D., & Greenberg, J. (1988). *The measurement of boundary ambiguity in families: Research instrument* (Family Social Science Department, University of Minnesota). St. Paul, MN: Agricultural Extension Service.

Boss, P. G., & Weiner, J. P. (1988). Rethinking assumptions about women's development and family therapy. In C. J. Falicov (Ed.), *Family transitions: Continuity and change over the life cycle.* New York: Guilford Press.

Boss, P. G., & Whitaker, C. (1979). Dialogue on separation: Clinicians as educators. *Family Coordinator, 28*(3).

Bourne, P. G. (1969). *The psychology and physiology of stress.* New York: Academic Press.

Brown, B. B. (1980). Perspectives on social stress. In H. Selye (Ed.), *Selye's guide to stress research.* New York: Van Nostrand Reinhold.

Brubaker, T. (1985). *Later life families.* Beverly Hills, CA: Sage.

Bruhn, J. G., Chandler, B., Miller, M. C., Wolfe, S., & Lynn, T. N. (1966). Social aspects of coronary heart disease in two adjacent ethnically different communities. *American Journal of Public Health, 56,* 1493-1506.

Buckley, W. (1967). *Sociology and modern systems theory.* Englewood Cliffs, NJ: Prentice-Hall.

Burgess, E. (Ed.). (1968). *The urban community.* New York: Greenwood Press. (Original work published 1926)

Burr, W. (1973). *Theory construction and the sociology of the family.* New York: John Wiley.

Burr, W., Leigh, G., Day, R., & Constantine, J. (1979). Symbolic interaction and the family. In W. Burr, R. Hill, F. I. Nye, & I. Reiss (Eds.), *Contemporary theories about the family* (Vol. 2, pp. 42-111). New York: Free Press.

Caplan, G. (Ed.). (1961). *Prevention of marital disorders in children.* New York: Basic Books.

Caplan, G. (1964). *Principles of preventive psychiatry.* New York: Basic Books.

Caplan, G. (1981). Mastery and stress: Psychological aspects. *American Journal of Psychiatry, 138*(4), 413-420.

Carter, E., & McGoldrick, M. (1980). *The family life cycle: A framework for family therapy.* New York: Gardner Press.

Cavan, R. S. (1959). Unemployment: Crisis of the common man. *Marriage and Family Living, 21,*139-146.

Cavan, R. S., & Ranck, K. H. (1938). *The family and the Depression.* Chicago: University of Chicago Press.

Cobb, S. (1974). A model for life events and their consequences. In B. S. Dohrenwend & B. P. Dohrenwend (Eds.), *Stressful life events: Their nature and effects.* New York: John Wiley.

Coelho, G., Hamburg, D., & Adams, J. (Eds.). (1974). *Coping and adaptation.* New York: Basic Books.

Cohen, F. (1975). *Psychological preparation, coping, and recovery from surgery.* Unpublished doctoral dissertation, University of California, Berkeley.

Danieli, Y. (1985). The treatment and prevention of long-term effects and intergenerational transmission of victimization: A lesson from Holocaust survivors and their children. In C. Figley (Ed.), *Trauma and its wake* (pp. 295-313). New York: Brunner/Mazel.

Davis, E. L., & Boss, P. G. (1980). *Rural divorce: How rural wives cope with separation* (Technical report). Madison: University of Wisconsin, Department of Child and Family Studies.

DeBeauvoir, S. (1953). *The second sex.* New York: Alfred A. Knopf.

Dohrenwend, B. S., & Dohrenwend, B. P. (1974). *Stressful life events: Their nature and effects.* New York: John Wiley.

Dowling, C. (1981). *The Cinderella complex.* New York: Summit Books.

Dumon, W. (1980). *Committee on Family Research Gazette, 8*(3). Leuven, Belgium: International Sociological Association.

Elder, G. H. (1974). *Children of the Great Depression.* Chicago: University of Chicago Press.

Elder, G. H., & Rockwell, R. C. (1979). The life-course and human development: An ecological perspective. *International Journal of Behavioral Development, 2,* 1-21.

Erikson, E. (1950). *Childhood and society.* New York: W. W. Norton.

Feldman, S., & McCarthy, F. E. (1983). National trends affecting disaster response and family organization in Bangladesh. In O. Hultaker & J. Trost (Eds.), *International Journal of Mass Emergencies and Disasters, 1*(1), 105-124.

Festinger, L. (1957). *A theory of cognitive dissonance.* Stanford, CA: Stanford University Press.

Field, H. S., & Bienen, L. B. (1980). *Jurors and rape.* Lexington, MA: Lexington Books.

Figley, C. (Ed.). (1978). *Stress disorders among Vietnam veterans.* New York: Brunner/Mazel.

Figley, C. (Ed.). (1980). *Mobilization: Part I. The Iranian crisis. Final report of The Task Force on Families of Catastrophe.* West Lafayette, IN: Purdue University Family Research Institute.

Figley, C. (Ed.). (1985). *Trauma and its wake.* New York: Brunner/Mazel.

Figley, C. R., & McCubbin, H. I. (1983). *Stress and the family: Vol. 2. Coping with catastrophe.* New York: Brunner/Mazel.

Fossum, M. A., & Mason, M. J. (1986). *Facing shame.* New York: W. W. Norton.

French, M. (1977). *The women's room.* New York: Summit Books.

Frey, F. W. (1963). Surveying peasant attitudes in Turkey. *Public Opinion Quarterly, 27,* 335-355.

Friedan, B. (1963). *The feminine mystique.* New York: W. W. Norton.

Gelles, R. (1979). *Family violence.* Beverly Hills, CA: Sage.

Gelles, R., & Cornell, C. (1986). *Intimate violence in families.* Beverly Hills, CA: Sage.

George, L. (1980). *Role transitions in later life.* Belmont, CA.: Brooks/Cole.

Gilligan, C. (1985). *In a different voice.* Cambridge, MA: Harvard University Press.

Gilligan, C. (1986). Exit-voice dilemmas in adolescent development. In A. Foxley, M. McPherson, & G. O'Donnell (Eds.), *Development, democracy, and the art of trespassing: Essays in honor of Albert O. Hirschman.* South Bend, IN: Notre Dame University Press.

Goffman, E. J. (1959). *The presentation of self in everyday life.* Garden City, NY: Doubleday.

Golan, N. (1978). *Treatment in crisis situations.* New York: Free Press.

Goldberger, L., & Breznitz, S. (Eds.). (1982). *Handbook of stress: Theoretical and clinical aspects.* New York: Free Press.

Goldenson, R. M. (1984). *Longman dictionary of psychology and psychiatry.* New York: Longman Press.

Goldner, V. (1985). Feminism and family therapy. *Family Process, 24*(2), 31-47.

Gonzalez, S., & Reiss, D. (1981). *Families and chronic illness: Technical difficulties in assessing adjustment.* Paper presented at the annual meeting of the National Council on Family Relations, Milwaukee.

Gonzalez, S., Reiss, D., & Kramer, N. (1986). Family process, chronic illness, and death: On the weakness of strong bonds. *Archives of General Psychiatry, 43,* 795-804.

Guntern, G. (1979). *Social change, stress and mental health in the pearl of the Alps.* New York: Springer-Verlag.

Gurman, A., & Kniskern, D. (1986). Research on the process and outcome of marital and family therapy. In S. Garfield & A. Bergin (Eds.), *Handbook of psychotherapy and behavioral change* (3rd ed.). New York: John Wiley.

Hall, R. C., & Malone, P. O. (1974). Psychiatric residuals of prolonged captivity experience. In H. I. McCubbin, E. Hunter, & B. Dahl (Eds.), *Families of prisoners of*

war and servicemen missing in action. San Diego, CA: Center for Prisoner of War
Studies, Naval Health Research Center.

Hamburg, D. A., & Adams, J. E. (1967). A perspective on coping: Seeking and utilizing
information in major transitions. *Archives of General Psychiatry, 17,* 277-284.

Hansen, D., & Hill, R. (1964). Families under stress. In H. T. Christensen (Ed.),
Handbook of marriage and the family. Chicago: Rand McNally.

Hare-Musten, R. (1978). A feminist approach to family therapy. *Family Process, 17*(4),
181-194.

Henry, J. P., & Stephen, P. M. (1977). *Stress, health and the social environment: A
sociobiologic approach to medicine.* New York: Springer-Verlag.

Hilberg, R. (1961). *The destruction of the European Jews.* New York: Harper & Row.

Hildebrand, J. (1987, July 13). Bully behavior not just part of growing up. *Minneapolis
Star and Tribune,* pp. 1C-2C.

Hill, R. (1958, February-March). Generic features of families under stress. *Social
Casework, 49,* 139-150.

Hill, R. (1971). *Families under stress.* Westport, CT: Greenwood Press. (Original work
published 1949).

Hill, R. (1971, October). Modern systems theory and the family: A confrontation. *Social
Science Information, 3,* 7-26.

Hill, R. (1973). *Family life cycle: Critical role transitions.* Paper presented at the
Thirteenth International Family Research Seminar, Paris.

Hill, R., & Joy, C. (1979). *Conceptualizing and operationalizing category systems for
phasing of family development.* Unpublished manuscript, Family Study Center,
Department of Sociology, University of Minnesota.

Hofer, M. A., Wolff, C. T., Friedman, S. B., & Mason, J. W. (1972). A psychoendocrine
study of bereavement (Parts I and II). *Psychosomatic Medicine, 34,* 481-504.

Hoffman, L. (1981). *Foundations of family therapy.* New York: Basic Books.

Holmes, T. H., & Rahe, R. H. (1967, September). The social readjustment rating scale.
Journal of Psychosomatic Research, 11, 213-218.

Hunter, E. J. (1983). Treating the military captive family. In F. Kaslow & R. Ridenour
(Eds.), *The military family: Dynamics and treatment.* New York: Guilford Press.

Insel, P. M., & Moos, R. H. (Eds.). (1974). *Health and the social environment.* Lexington,
MA: Lexington Books.

Janoff-Bulman, R. (1985). The aftermath of victimization: Rebuilding shattered assumptions. In C. Figley (Ed.), *Trauma and its wake* (pp. 15-35). New York: Brunner/Mazel.

Janoff-Bulman, R., & Frieze, I. H. (1983). Reactions to victimization [Special issue].
Journal of Social Issues, 39(2).

Kagitcibasi, C. (1983). How does the traditional family in Turkey cope with disasters? In
O. Hultaker & J. Trost (Eds.), *International Journal of Mass Emergencies and
Disasters, 1*(1), 145-152.

Kellam, S. G., Ensminger, M. E., & Turner, R. J. (1977, September). Family structure and
the mental health of children. *Archives of General Psychiatry, 34,* 1012-1022.

Kelly, W. E. (Ed.). (1985). *Post-traumatic stress disorder and the war veteran patient.*
New York: Brunner/Mazel.

Kiritz, S., & Moos, R. H. (1974). Psychological effects of social environments.
Psychosomatic Medicine, 36, 96-114.

Klein, D., & Hill, R. (1979). Determinants of problem-solving effectiveness. In W. Burr, R.
Hill, F. I. Nye, & I. Reiss (Eds.), *Contemporary theories about the family* (Vol. 1). New
York: Free Press.

Kluckhohn, F. R., & Strodtbeck, F. L. (1961). *Variations in value orientation.* Westport,
CT: Greenwood Press.

Kolbenschlag, M. (1979). *Kiss Sleeping Beauty Goodbye.* Garden City, NY: Doubleday.

Komarovsky, M. (1940). *The unemployed man and his family.* New York: Dryden Press.

Koos, E. L. (1946). *Families in trouble.* New York: King's Crown Press.

Kübler-Ross, E. (1969). *On death and dying.* New York: Macmillan.

Kutash, I. L., Schlesinger, L. B., & Associates (Eds.). (1980). *Handbook on stress and anxiety.* San Francisco: Jossey-Bass.

Laing, R. D. (1969). *The politics of the family.* New York: Pantheon.

LaVee, Y., McCubbin, H. I., & Patterson, J. (1985). The double ABCX model of family stress and adaptation: An empirical test by analysis of structural equations with latent variables. *Journal of Marriage and the Family, 47*(4), 811-826.

Lawrence, D. (1986, June 29). A soldier's parade and a supreme wrong. *Minneapolis Star and Tribune,* p. 17A.

Lazarus, R. S. (1966). *Psychological stress and the coping process.* New York: McGraw-Hill.

Lazarus, R. S. (1976). *Patterns of adjustment* (3rd ed.). New York: McGraw- Hill.

Lazarus, R. S. (1977). Cognitive and coping processes in emotion. In A. Monat & R. Lazarus (Eds.), *Stress and coping.* New York: Columbia University Press.

Lazarus, R. S., & Folkman, S. (1984). *Stress, appraisal, and coping.* New York: Springer.

Leik, R. K., Leik, S. A., Ekker, K., & Gifford, G. A. (1982, February). *Under the threat of Mt. St. Helens: A study of chronic family stress* (Final report for Federal Emergency Management Agency). Washington, DC: Office of Prevention, National Institute of Mental Health.

Lerner, M. J. (1971). Justice, guilt, and veridical perception. *Journal of Personality and Social Psychology, 20,* 127-135.

Lerner, M. J., & Simmons, C. (1966). Observers' reaction to the innocent victim: Compassion or rejection? *Journal of Personality and Social Psychology, 4,* 203-210.

Lieberman, E. (1971). American families and the Vietnam War. *Journal of Marriage and the Family, 33,* 709-721.

Lindemann, E. (1977). *Symptomatology and management of acute grief.* Paper presented at the centenary meeting of the American Psychiatric Association, Philadelphia, Penn., May 15-18, 1944. Reprinted in A. Monat & R. S. Lazarus (Eds.), *Stress and coping: An anthology.* New York: Columbia University Press.

Marris, P. (1974). *Loss and change.* New York: Random House.

McCabe, M. (1981). *Coping with divorce in an urban environment.* Unpublished doctoral dissertation, University of Wisconsin.

McCubbin, H. (1979, August). Integrating coping behavior in family stress theory. *Journal of Marriage and the Family, 41,* 237-244.

McCubbin, H. I., & Boss, P. G. (Eds.). (1980). Family stress, coping and adaptation. *Family Relations, 29*(4).

McCubbin, H., Boss, P. G., Wilson, L., & Lester, G. (1980). Developing family invulnerability to stress: Coping patterns and strategies wives employ. In J. Trost (Ed.), *The family and change.* Sweden: International Library.

McCubbin, H., Dahl, B., & Hunter, E. (1976). Research on the military family: A review. In H. McCubbin, B. Dahl, & E. Hunter (Eds.), *Families in the military system.* Beverly Hills, CA.: Sage.

McCubbin, H., Dahl, B., Lester, G., & Boss, P. G. (1975). *Coping with Separation Inventory (CSI).* San Diego, CA: Naval Health Research Center.

McCubbin, H. I., & Figley, C. R. (1983). *Stress and the family: Vol. 1. Coping with normative transitions.* New York: Brunner/Mazel.

McCubbin, H., Joy, C., Cauble, B., Comeau, J., Patterson, J., & Needle, R. (1980). Family stress and coping: A decade review. *Journal of Marriage and the Family, 42*(4), 855-871.

McCubbin, H., Patterson, J., & Wilson, L. (1981). *Family Inventory of Life Events and Changes (FILE): Research instrument.* St. Paul: Family Social Science, University of Minnesota.

McCubbin, H., Sussman, M., & Patterson, J. (Eds.). (1983a). *Advances in family stress theory and research.* New York: Haworth Press.

McCubbin, H., Sussman, M., & Patterson, J. (Eds.). (1983b). *Social stress and the family.* New York: Haworth Press.

McFarlane, P. T., & Sussman, M. B. (1982, April). *Residential relocation and family stress.* University of Delaware, Department of Individual and Family Studies.

Mechanic, D. (1978). *Students under stress: A study in the social psychology of adaptation.* Madison: University of Wisconsin Press.

Mederer, H., & Hill, R. (1983). Critical transitions over the family life span: Theory and research. In H. McCubbin, M. Sussman, & J. Patterson (Eds.), *Social stress and the family.* New York: Haworth Press.

Menaghan, E. G. (1983). Individual coping efforts and family studies: Conceptual and methodological issues. In H. I. McCubbin, M. B. Sussman, & J. M. Patterson (Eds.), *Social stress and the family.* New York: Haworth Press.

Miller, A. (1986). *Thou shalt not be aware.* New York: Meridian.

Monat, A., & Lazarus, R. (Eds.). (1977). *Stress and coping.* New York: Columbia University Press.

Moore vs. City of East Cleveland, Ohio (1977). 413 U.S. 494.

Moos, R. H., & Billings, A. G. (1981). Conceptualizing and measuring coping resources and processes. In L. Goldberger & S. Breznitz (Eds.), *Handbook of stress: Theoretical and clinical aspects.* New York: Macmillan.

Moos, R. H., Finney, J., & Chan, D. (1981). The process of recovery from alcoholism: Comparing alcoholic patients and matched community controls. *Journal of Studies on Alcohol, 42,* 383-402.

Neugarten, B., & Hagestad, G. (1977). Age and the life course. In R. H. Binstock & E. Shanas (Eds.), *Handbook on aging and the social sciences.* New York: Van Nostrand Reinhold.

Nuttal, R. L. (1980). *Coping with catastrophe: Family adjustments to national disaster.* Keynote address at Groves Conference on Marriage and the Family, Gatlinburg, TN.

Olson, D. H., McCubbin, H. I., Barnes, H., Larsen, A., Muxen, M., & Wilson, M. (1983). *Families: What makes them work.* Beverly Hills, CA: Sage.

Overmier, J. B., & Seligman, M. E. P. (1967). Effects of inescapable shock upon subsequent escape and avoidance learning. *Journal of Comparative and Physiological Psychology, 63,* 23-33.

Palgi, P. (1970). The adaptability and vulnerability of family types in the changing Israeli society. In A. Jarvus & J. Marcus (Eds.), *Children and families in Israel.* New York: Gordon & Breech.

Palgi, P. (1973). Socio-cultural expressions and implications of death, mourning, and bereavement. In E. Palgi (Ed.), *Israel arising out of the war situation.* Israel: Jerusalem Academic Press.

Palgi, P. (1975). *Culture and mourning: Expressions of bereavement arising out of the war situation in Israel.* Paper presented at the International Conference on Psychological Stress and Adjustment in Time of War and Peace, Tel Aviv, Israel.

Papalia, D. E., & Olds, S. W. (1986). *Human development.* New York: McGraw-Hill.

Parsons, T., & Bales, R. F. (1955). *The family socialization and interaction process.* Glencoe, IL: Free Press.

Pearlin, L. I., & Leiberman, M. A. (1979). Social sources of emotional distress. In R. G. Simmons (Ed.), *Research in community mental health.* Greenwich, CT: JAI Press.

Pearlin, L. I., Menaghan, E. G., Lieberman, M. A., & Mullan, J. T. (1981). The stress process. *Journal of Health and Social Behavior, 22*(4), 337-356.

Pearlin, L. I., & Radebaugh, C. W. (1976). Economic strains and the coping functions of alcohol. *American Journal of Sociology, 82,* 652-663.

Peterson, L., & Seligman, M. (1983). Learned helplessness and victimization. *Journal of Social Issues, 39*(2), 105-118.

Phillemer, K. A. & Wolf, R. S. (Eds.). (1986). *Elder abuse.* Dover, MA: Auburn House.

Pogrebin, L. C. (1983). *Family politics.* New York: McGraw-Hill.

Pollner, M., & McDonald-Wikler, L. (1985). The social construction of unreality: A case study of a family's attribution of competence to a severely retarded child. *Family Process, 24*(2), 241-254.

Price, V. A. (1982). *Type A behavior pattern.* New York: Academic Press.

Rahe, R. (1974). The pathway between subjects' recent life changes and their near-future illness reports: Representative results and methodological issues. In B. S. Dohrenwend & B. P. Dohrenwend (Eds.), *Stressful life events.* New York: John Wiley.

Rapoport, L. (1965). The state of crisis: Some theoretical considerations. In H. Parad (Ed.), *Crisis intervention: Selected readings.* New York: Family Service Association of America.

Reiss, D. (1981). *The family's construction of reality.* Cambridge, MA: Harvard University Press.

Reiss, D., & Oliver, M. E. (1983). Family stress as community frame. In H. I. McCubbin, M. B. Sussman, & J. M. Patterson (Eds.), *Social stress and the family.* New York: Haworth Press.

Riegel, K. (1979). *Foundations of dialectical psychology.* New York: Academic Press.

Russell, C. (1974, May). Transition to parenthood. *Journal of Marriage and the Family, 36,* 294-302.

Russell, D. E. H. (1982, March). *Rape, child sexual abuse, and sexual harassment in the workplace: An analysis of the prevalence, cause, and recommended solution.* Final report presented to the California Commission on Crime Control and Violence Prevention, Sacramento.

Scherz, F. H. (1966). Family treatment concepts. *Social Casework, 47*(4), 234-240.

Selye, H. (1978). *The stress of life* (rev. ed.). New York: McGraw-Hill.

Selye, H. (Ed.). (1980). *Selye's guide to stress research* (Vol. 1). New York: Van Nostrand Reinhold.

Sid and Nancy: Gruesome, gross, and engrossing. (1987, January 2). *Minneapolis Star and Tribune,* p. 4C.

Sontag, S. (1979). *Illness as a metaphor.* New York: Vintage Books.

Stinnett, N., & DeFrain, J. (1986). *Secrets of strong families.* New York: Berkeley Books.

Thorne, B., & Yalom, M. (Eds.). (1982). *Rethinking the family.* New York: Longman.

Vaillant, G. E. (1977). *Adaptation to life.* Boston: Little, Brown.

Vaughn, B. E., Egeland, B., Sroufe, L. A., & Waters, E. (1979). Individual differences in infant-mother attachment at twelve and eighteen months: Stability and change in families under stress. *Child Development, 50,* 971-975.

Ventura, J., & Boss, P. G. (1983, November). The Family Coping Inventory applied to parents with new babies. *Journal of Marriage and the Family, 45*(4), 867-875.

Walker, A. (1985). Reconceptualizing family stress. *Journal of Marriage and the Family, 47*(4), 827-837.

Watts, W. A. (1984). Designing attitude change programs. In R. Jones (Ed.), *Special education in transition: Attitudes toward the handicapped.* Reston, VA: Council for Exceptional Children.

Watzlawick, P., Weakland, J., & Fisch, R. (1974). *Change: Principles of problem formation and problem resolution.* New York: W. W. Norton.

Wegner, J. R. (1982). The status of women in Jewish and Islamic marriage and divorce law. *Harvard Women's Law Journal, 5*, 1-32.

Weiner, J. P. & Boss, P. G. (1985). Exploring gender bias against women: Ethics for marriage and family therapy [Special issue]. *Counseling and Values, 30*(1).

Wikler, L. (1981). Chronic stresses of families of mentally retarded children. *Family Relations, 30*(2), 281-288.

Wolff, C. T., Friedman, S. B., Hofer, M. A., & Mason, J. W. (1964). Relationship between psychological defenses and mean urinary 17-hydroxycortocasteroid excretion rates: A predictive study of parents of fatally ill children. *Psychosomatic Medicine, 26*, 576-591.

Index

About the Author

Pauline Boss is a Professor in the Department of Family Social Science at the University of Minnesota. She has been a professor at the University of Minnesota since 1981 and, before that, at the University of Wisconsin—Madison. She received her doctorate in child development and family studies from the University of Wisconsin—Madison in 1975. Since 1973, she has conducted research on family stress, especially when a family member's absence is ambiguous. She is currently principal investigator of a National Institute of Aging research project titled "The Psycho-Social Impact of Dementia on Family and Caregiver." Her previous research has been on families of men declared missing in action and families of rural and urban midlife families when an adolescent has just left home.

She is a member of the National Council on Family Relations (NCFR), a charter member of the American Family Therapy Association (AFTA), a clinical member and fellow of the American Association of Marriage and Family Therapists (AAMFT), and has served as president of the Groves Conference on Marriage and the Family from 1984 to 1987. She has been elected by her peers as chair of the Research Committee of AAMFT, chair of the NCFR Research and Theory Section, chair of the 1984 NCFR Theory and Methods Workshop, and program chair for the 1986 Annual Conference of NCFR.

In 1983, she was elected to Fellowship by the American Association of Marital and Family Therapists for "significant contribution to the field of marital and family therapy as a researcher, teacher, and supervisor." She continues her work as a family scientist and as a family therapist at the University of Minnesota.